READING
WITHOUT
NONSENSE

4th Edition

Other Books by Frank Smith

Understanding Reading (six editions)
Writing and the Writer (two editions)
Comprehension and Learning
Insult to Intelligence
*Whose Language? What Power?**
*to think**
*The Book of Learning and Forgetting**
*The Glass Wall**
Ourselves: Why We Are Who We Are

ESSAYS

Essays Into Literacy
Joining the Literacy Club
Between Hope and Havoc
Unspeakable Acts, Unnatural Practices

EDITED VOLUMES

The Genesis of Language (with George A. Miller)
Psycholinguistics and Reading
Awakening to Literacy (with Hillel Goelman and Antoinette A. Oberg)

---

* Also published by Teachers College Press

READING
WITHOUT
NONSENSE

4th Edition

Frank Smith

Teachers College, Columbia University
New York and London

Published by Teachers College Press, 1234 Amsterdam Avenue, New York, NY 10027

Library of Congress Cataloging-in-Publication Data

Smith, Frank, 1928–
    Reading without nonsense / Frank Smith.–4th ed.
        p. cm.
    Includes index.
    ISBN-13: 978-0-8077-4686-8 (pbk.)
    ISBN-10: 0-8077-4686-X (pbk.)
        1. Reading. I. Title.

    LB1050.S5732 2006
    428.4–dc22   2005052843

ISBN-13 978-0-8077-4686-8 (paper)   ISBN-10 0-8077-4686-X (paper)

Printed on acid-free paper

Manufactured in the United States of America

13   12   11   10   09   08   8   7   6   5   4   3   2

Contents

Preface to the 4th Edition

What has happened in the past 7 years to justify a revised edition of *Reading Without Nonsense?*

Certainly nothing about reading has changed. We still read in the same way that we have for millennia, even if we spend more time reading from electronic devices. We still have the same eyes, the same brains, and we learn and understand the world in the same way.

And certainly we have no new understanding of reading. Science has not been able to uncover anything new about the way people read; as always, people are using their eyes and their brains to make sense of visible language.

What *has* changed is the way reading is taught, or rather the political and commercial attitudes toward the way reading should be taught.

Once it was believed that reading was a matter of getting meaning from print, either directly or by decoding printed words to sound. In earlier editions I have shown that the decoding view can only engage learners in meaningless and distracting activities, making learning to read more difficult. Today there is an official consensus that decoding to sound is the *only* route to reading, and if decoding doesn't work, it is because children are inadequate in some way and should pay more attention to spoken language.

There's a lot more coercion today, led by federal government agencies, with teachers being mandated to follow commercial programs that emphasize the decoding approach. This approach is supposed to be "scientific" and "research-based," even though it is contrary to evidence, observation, reason, and the experience of many teachers.

In particular, all this mindless intrusion into classrooms and children's lives is necessary, it is claimed, because reading is an unnatural activity. Spoken language is natural, and we can leave it to children to learn it for themselves. But because written language is unnatural, we have to engage children in all kinds of unnatural, nonsensical, and confusing exercises if they are to learn to read. The very idea is absurd, but it is widespread.

This is what makes the 4th edition of this book necessary: to show that reading is natural, something that no one would have dreamed would be a significant issue 7 years ago. Not everyone will learn to read when we want them to and in the way we often want them to, but those natural individual differences have nothing to do with whether or not the act of reading is natural. They should never be justification for engaging any learner, of any age, in meaningless, bewildering, and discouraging activities. Learning to read should always make sense.

For those involved in teaching reading, I show in this book that it is only through reading that children learn to read, and that parents and teachers must therefore ensure that reading is always accessible and enjoyable for every learner. In particular, I show that children can learn to read only through materials and activities that they understand and are interested in and that they can relate to what they already know. Anything they can't relate to what they already know will be nonsense to them, whether or not it seems to make sense to the adult. Expecting children to learn to read through nonsense is the surest method of making learning to read impossible. The emphasis of this book is on what teachers should be sensitive to rather than on what they should do.

Extensive research in many cultures continues to confirm what countless parents and experienced teachers have known intuitively: Children become readers when they are engaged in unthreatening situations where written language is meaningfully used, much the way they learn spoken language from their association with people around them who use speech in meaningful ways. Learning is a constant endeavor to make sense, and the effort to teach or to inform must therefore always endeavor to be interesting and comprehensible. I continue to hope that this book will be interesting and comprehensible to everyone concerned with literacy, be they practicing teachers, students and faculty in colleges of education, parents, administrators, trustees, or individuals concerned with their own reading.

THE ROUTE THROUGH THE BOOK

Chapter 1: The Most Natural Act in the World. Reading is usually discussed and taught as if it were self-contained, with no connection to anything else that people do. But if it is to be properly understood, reading must be placed in a much broader context.

Chapter 2: Learning to Be a Reader. Not only reading, but learning to read, is a natural and far more general phenomenon.

Chapter 3: The Limitations of Phonics. To many people, phonics is synonymous with reading. But phonics is one approach to instruction out of many, and is far removed from reading itself.

Chapter 4: Reading—From Behind the Eyes. This is the important side of reading, where every instructional approach has to make sense.

Chapter 5: Bottlenecks of Memory. Both reading and teaching reading must respect the strengths and weaknesses of memory.

Chapter 6: Language and Meaning. Neither reading nor teaching reading can be regarded as mechanical or rote activities. Sense is always significant and must be predominant.

Chapter 7: Constructing a Theory of the World. Sense should never be taken for granted. We all have to make sense of every connection we make with the world, including every aspect of reading.

Chapter 8: Letters, Words, and Meanings. Like everything else, reading is a matter of choices. This chapter examines the consequences of choosing letters, words, or sense as a focus of teaching reading.

Chapter 9: Joining the Club of Readers. Reading is much more than interaction with print. It is a matter of self-image, of who learners see themselves as being.

Chapter 10: The Importance of Teachers. The fact that so much of reading depends on the state of mind of the learner enhances rather than diminishes the significance of sensitive and autonomous teachers.

Chapter 11: Labels and Fables. Learning to read would be much easier for many students if there were fewer myths and false categorizations around, which add to the nonsense that surrounds reading.

NOTE ABOUT REFERENCES

I have refrained from overburdening the text of this book with detailed references, footnotes, or theoretical debate. My aim is readability. Technical discussions, supporting arguments, and copious references can all be found in my more specialized books: *Understanding Reading* (6th ed., 2004), and *Writing and the Writer* (2nd ed., 1994), both published by Lawrence Erlbaum Associates, Mahwah, NJ.

READING
WITHOUT
NONSENSE

4th Edition

CHAPTER 1

The Most Natural Act in the World

Throughout this book I emphasize that there is nothing special, unique, or mysterious about reading. Reading doesn't call upon us to do anything different from what we are doing all the time we are awake. Reading is the most natural activity in the world, something we all do constantly, without conscious effort, whether or not we are literate.

Check the dictionary. *Reading* is defined as "interpreting"—making sense of something, predicting, or anticipating. Reading print is only a small part of this. In its broadest sense, reading is striving to understand everything in the world around us in which we are particularly interested and involved. Golfers read greens (my dictionary tells me), and canoeists read rapids. Sailors and farmers read weather. We read minds, faces, palms, body language, animal tracks, clouds, maps, music, mathematics, and between the lines. People have tried to read portents in everything from tea leaves to intestines. Reading written language is only a special use of the term for particular situations, it is not a special kind of activity. Reading, in the literacy sense, is not rocket science.

Reading is *the* fundamental human activity. Everything we do depends on the way we make sense of the world and our place in it. Unless we can read the situation we are in, there is no reason for doing anything. Being unable to read the situation we are in can be mildly irritating or intriguing—when we have no idea where to go in a maze or a crossword puzzle. But it can also be deeply disturbing and even horrifying when we have no idea of what is going on.

Even when we restrict the word *reading* to its most common use—making sense of print—there is nothing distinctive about the activity in the structure or functions of the brain. Despite diagrams that sometimes appear in textbooks and in popular articles, allocating specific functions to particular locations in the brain, reading isn't the exclusive concern of any one part. Surgeons and scientists have yet to isolate a specialized "reading center" in the brain. Many areas of the brain are active when we read, some may even be essential, but none is involved with reading to the exclusion of anything else. Illness or injury may occasionally affect the working of the brain so that ability to read is disturbed, but almost certainly some more general activity involving either language or vision will also be impaired.

There is also nothing unique about reading as far as the intellect is concerned. From a language point of view, reading makes no demands that the brain doesn't meet in the comprehension of speech. And visually, there is nothing in reading that the eyes and brain don't accomplish when we look around a room to locate an object or to distinguish one face from another.

AN UNDEFINING MOMENT

It is pointless to look for a simple definition of reading, even in the strictly literacy sense. Reading is no different from all the other common words in our language in having a multiplicity of meanings. And since the meaning of the word on any particular occasion will depend largely on the context in which it occurs, we shouldn't expect that a single definition for reading will be found, let alone one that will throw light on its nature. One can't even ask such a "straightforward" question as whether reading necessarily entails understanding.

If we recommend that a friend read a particular book, we obviously intend the friend to understand it. It would be redundant to the point of rudeness to say we wanted the book to be read and understood. But, on the other hand, it would be quite reasonable for the friend to reply, "Well, I've already read the book and I couldn't understand it." We couldn't object that the friend hadn't read the book just because it wasn't understood. So the word *reading* may sometimes entail understanding, and sometimes not, and any dispute about whether reading does or doesn't necessarily entail understanding is a dispute about language, not about the nature of reading. To avoid endless semantic arguments—which are especially frustrating when we don't realize that we are involved in one—we should stop looking for definitions of reading and consider instead what is involved in reading. Illustration, description, and analysis are, after all, what we usually want when we ask people to define their terms.

There is one thing we can say reading is *not*—and that is a nonsensical activity. Reading is the antithesis of nonsense; it strives always to find and make sense. Nonsense is naturally ignored. That is why it is amazing, and demands explanation, that so much reading instruction is nonsensical.

THE RANGE OF READING

Consider the different ways in which reading may take place, from the public recital of poetry or political agendas to the private scrutiny of literary works, price lists, transportation timetables, and the stock market. A list of some of the different sorts of things that people can be called upon to read might perhaps sensitize us to the risk of regarding reading too narrowly. I'm not suggesting that there are many different kinds of reading, or that we are doing something radically different when we read poetry instead of price lists. But reflecting upon the range of reading will show the inadequacy of definitions of reading as "the identification of written words" or "the apprehension of the author's thoughts," neither of which would seem to apply to all the words we skip on the way to the number we are trying to find in a telephone directory. On the other hand, anything that we can discover that the range of reading situations have in common will surely give us a clue to the central factors in reading.

In education, particularly, reading is often perceived extremely narrowly, either in terms of exercises that learners may be required to give their attention to or in terms of books—and often only "great books" at that. To some educators, the sole purpose of reading would seem to be participation in the wisdom and delights of great literature (an emphasis that can put many individuals off serious reading for life). The development of children's reading ability may be judged in terms of the number of items of "children's literature" they have read.

But there are other kinds of books apart from literature, apart from stories even, and apart from all the poetry and plays that are also found in print. There are all the textbooks and technical works that one might read for specific information, and many other books that are skimmed rather than studied for reference rather than total immersion. There are books that no one would consider reading from cover to cover—dictionaries, directories, encyclopedias, timetables, catalogs, registers, and bibliographies. And, for all their variety, books constitute only a small part of our daily reading fare. Most of us read newspapers, with their headlines, articles, picture captions, sports scores, weather forecasts, stock market summaries, entertainment guides, and advertisements. The mail brings letters, forms, bills, magazines, journals, and more advertisements. There is print of all kinds on computer monitors, much of it unwanted. There is print on television and print in the television guide. At the cinema there are the credits, and at the theater the program. Every product has its label—and its promotional materials. We read signs in stores and billboards outside, traffic signs, street signs, destination signs, operating instructions, assembly directions, menus, recipes, knitting patterns, computer programs, chemical formulas, and the formal expressions of logic and algebra. Some of us read special scripts, such as shorthand, Morse, Braille, or the sign languages of the deaf.

Is there anything that all these literacy aspects of reading have in common, together with the more general kinds of reading that I have referred to, like reading minds, faces, and the weather?

READING—GETTING QUESTIONS ANSWERED

One of the most common answers to the question of what reading is—the decoding of written words by producing the sounds of letters of the alphabet—fails with respect to many of the examples I have given. If we utter or mutter a word at all while we are searching through a dictionary or telephone directory, it is likely to be the word we are looking for, not the word we are looking at. Besides, I spend a large part of this book (particularly Chapter 3) demonstrating that decoding to sound rarely works and can be catastrophic in its effect on learning to read.

With dictionaries and directories it would also seem to be stretching a point to say that *reading* is "understanding the author's thoughts," a definition that similarly appears to have minimal relevance to reading street signs and package labels. Moreover, definitions like "understanding print" or "engaging in communication" can hardly be said to explain reading; the problem of how the reader understands the print or achieves the communication remains. We are still left with the question of what the reader actually does.

A rather imposing technical definition of *reading* is "extracting information from text," which perhaps goes a little way toward putting reading into a clearer perspective but still ignores much of the problem.

Obviously, getting information is something that is involved in all the different reading situations that I have listed—if you can read, you can get information from directories and menus and street signs and record labels as well as from textbooks and novels—but there is a lot of information in much of this print that we don't get, for the very good reason that we don't want it. The telephone directory is bursting with information about people we never want to call. The daily newspaper is replete with information, from the publisher's name to the most esoteric small ad, deliberately ignored by most of us most of the time. Even when we read a novel, we are unlikely to pay attention to all the information that is available in the text.

As I explain later in the book, undue concern with all the "visual information" that lies in print—with what is in front of the eyes—can only interfere with reading. Fluent readers are those who restrict their attention to aspects of print that are most relevant to their purposes. It is indeed true that we extract information from print when we read, but very selectively. The basic skill of reading lies more in what is going on behind the eyes—in the reader's mind—than in the visual stimulation that bombards us from the print.

Any definition of reading should recognize the selective way in which we read all kinds of print—not striving mechanically to "extract" all the information made available to us, but deliberately seeking just the information that we need to answer specific questions that we are asking, like finding a route between two places on a map.

Here we have a conception of reading that does indeed cover all the different kinds of situations that I have listed: Reading is asking questions of a text. And reading with understanding becomes a matter of getting your questions answered. You are able to read a telephone directory when you can find the answer to your question about the number of the person you want to call. You can read a menu when you can find the information you seek about the lunchtime special. You can read a novel or textbook when you are able to get sufficient information from the print to leave you with no unanswered questions, no confusion or bewilderment. When you look at a street sign, you are asking, "What street am I on?" or, even more specifically, "Am I on the street I am looking for?" Even more general expressions like "reading faces" or "reading minds" may be characterized as asking questions and finding answers.

This tendency to ask specific questions when we look at something extends far beyond the reading of print. We would be constantly bewildered or surprised if we never had certain questions and expectations in mind. Even when we look at a watch or clock, we are likely to have a far more specific question in mind than "What time is it?" We want to know, "Is it time to go home yet?" or "Am I late for my next appointment?" The next few times you observe people looking at their watches, ask them what time it is. They will probably have to look at the watch again, for the simple reason that they didn't look to see what time it was, but whether or not it was some particular time they thought it might be.

THE STRATEGIES OF READING

This book will demonstrate that fluent readers can find answers in print to questions about sense or meaning without the prior identification of individual words or individual letters. Of course, if they can't achieve meaning directly, they may try to work it out from the individual words, just as they may try to identify an unfamiliar word from its individual letters. But both alternatives are largely impractical; they take too long and leave too much uncertainty. It is difficult to identify an unfamiliar word on the basis of its component letters because of the complexity and unreliability of rules for "sounding out," and it is almost impossible to work out the sense of a difficult sentence from the meanings of its component words because of the alternative meanings that individual words can have. In both cases, what makes meanings and individual words become obvious and meaningful is *context*, which means the general sense in which the difficult element is embedded. Provided that the text that readers are trying to interrogate has the overall possibility of making sense to them, the parts that are unfamiliar can usually be understood because of all the other clues to potential meaning that are available.

Reading directly for meaning, then, becomes the best strategy for reading—not as a consequence of reading words and letters, but as an alternative to the identification of individual words or letters. In each case we are looking at the same thing—the printed marks on a contrastive background—but asking a different question. We can look at the print and ask questions about letters, in which case we shall require a relatively concentrated amount of visual information and see very little.

Or we can look at the print and ask questions about words, in which case we see a little bit more but probably not enough to make sense of what we are trying to read. Or we can look at the print and ask questions about meaning, in which case we won't be aware of individual words but we shall have the best chance of reading fluently and meaningfully. Paradoxically enough, because we are concentrating on meaning, we have the best chance of getting individual words right, should we be reading aloud.

What kinds of question do we ask when we are reading for meaning? To answer that question I would have to recapitulate all the different reading situations listed a few paragraphs ago, and I would have to catalog the multiplicity of uses to which written language can be put. There is no simple answer because the questions readers ask depend precisely on the purpose of their reading in the first place. Except for rather obvious examples like looking up a particular telephone number or examining a menu or a street sign, it is unlikely that any two people would ever ask exactly the same question of the same text. That is why it would be unusual to get two identical interpretations—identical "readings"—of the same novel or poem.

Consider reading a menu. How often do we read a menu from top to bottom, left to right, noting every word, with no expectation of what we are likely to see and no particular interest in anything we might be likely to find out? We read menus with a purpose and examine them. We ask our questions selectively: "What's for dessert?" or, even more specifically, "Is there apple pie?" and our next question is possibly "What does it cost?" We know the information we want and we have a pretty good idea of where to look for it. We can predict the alternatives from which words and phrases on the menu are likely to be drawn. We could certainly predict many thousands of words most unlikely to occur, and indeed, we would be very surprised if any of these unlikely and therefore unpredicted words occurred. Since we have only a few alternatives in our mind—thanks to all the prior knowledge we bring to reading menus—very little visual information is required from the printed marks to give us our answers. A glance usually tells us what we want to know. (If we spend a lot of time looking at a menu, it's not because it takes a long time to read it but because we can't decide what to order.)

Suppose I am looking at a telephone directory to find the number of my friend Jack Jones. My first question as my eye runs down each column is "Jones?" (meaning "Is this word I am focusing on Jones?"). I need so little visual information to answer this question that I can run my eyes down columns of names at the rate of hundreds of lines a minute. When I find myself among the Joneses, my eye moves slightly to the right and my next question is "Jack?" followed by a check of middle initials and addresses. And when I find the Jones I want, the critical question becomes "What is the number?"—the answer to which is the only information I commit to memory. We don't read telephone directories as if they were menus, at least not if we are competent readers and comprehend what we are doing. The process of reading is basically the same in both instances—predicting and getting the answers to questions—but the situations differ because of the different questions that we ask. To repeat, if we don't know what questions to ask, then we don't comprehend—hence the difficulty I would have trying to find a number in the Tokyo telephone directory.

In reading a recipe, a knitting pattern, or instructions for assembling a bicycle, a preliminary question must often be "Where am I now?"— meaning "Where is the place that I have got to so far?" You will note that this quite specific question is not unlike the search for the name we want in a telephone directory or for a wanted word in a dictionary. The next question, to phrase it very loosely, is something like "What should I do now?"; but if we have any understanding of what we are doing, it is likely to be much more specific, something like "Should I add the eggs now or the butter?" or "Do I attach the ringbolt before the switch assembly?" If we don't understand what we are doing, if we have no expectation of what the next step is likely to be, then we are unlikely to understand the instructions, or even to be able to find our place in them. "What should I do now?" questions may sound very vague, but for comprehension to take place, there has to be a limited range of alternatives, both to ease the information-processing burden on the brain and to protect us from surprise and bewilderment.

When we come to consider more complex texts than menus and telephone directories—for example, newspaper and magazine articles, technical reports, and novels—it's not so easy even to illustrate what the questions might be. Many questions would differ from one novel to another, obviously depending on the characters and the plot; other questions would differ from one part to another of the same novel. Some questions might persist through long sections of a book—"Which suspect is the murderer?"—while others might not extend beyond a sentence—"Is the poison victim dead?" (You get through a novel by having current questions answered and moving on to the next question. If at any time you fail to find an answer that you need, you are likely to be confused and uncomprehending, but if you are left with no questions to ask, you will be either bewildered or bored.)

Possibly there are some basic questions that are part of our comprehension of all novels, but that issue seems to me part of a theory of literature, beyond any analysis of the basic processes of reading. Questions that some specialists think readers should ask about such recondite matters as style and technique—often to the perplexity of children at school—more properly fall within the province of literary criticism. Inference and judgment are often considered part of reading, and there is indeed a skill in looking for the evidence. But fundamentally, reading novels rests on the same basic process as any other form of reading: asking questions and knowing how to find the answers in the print.

I should emphasize that the questions we ask in reading are almost invariably implicit; we aren't usually aware of the questions or even that we are asking them. But the fact that we are unaware of the questions doesn't mean they aren't being asked. They are like the questions we ask in making sense of spoken language and of the world in general. We usually become aware of the need for such questions only when we lack them (and we're bewildered) or when they mislead us (and we're surprised).

Not only are we generally unaware of our questions as we read, we are also usually unaware that we are getting answers, and of how we find these answers in the print. We aren't aware of the process of finding and evaluating answers but only of the consequences of the process, the decisions made by the brain. We are aware of letters, or words, or general meaning, depending on what we are looking for.

These two closely related skills that we usually perform without awareness—asking appropriate questions and finding relevant answers—lie at the heart of reading. Yet these are not skills that are expressly taught. Indeed, it is difficult to see how anyone could claim to teach such skills since there is very little that can be said specifically about either the nature of the questions or the source of the answers. But then, it is obviously not necessary that these skills should be taught specifically since all of us have learned to read without the benefit of such instruction.

The implicit questions readers ask must vary with the material they are reading, which is why prior knowledge is so important. If we don't know the right questions to ask of a particular passage, then we won't be able to read it, no matter how hard we concentrate. Manuals for many electronic devices are notoriously difficult to read because they fail to provide answers to questions readers ask (or because readers don't ask the questions the manuals answer). And if children learning to read are confronted with material they can't possibly ask questions of—because they find it boring or beyond their understanding, or simply because it is unequivocal nonsense—then we shouldn't be surprised if they can't read. What questions could they be asking?

There are other critical aspects of reading, such as achieving the right balance of information from in front of the eyes and prior knowledge from behind them; not reading so slowly that short-term memory is overwhelmed; not trying to memorize so much that comprehension is affected; predicting; and learning to identify and understand unfamiliar words from context and from similarity to words already known. Readers even acquire a working understanding of the limitations of phonics: Rather than expecting to sound out unfamiliar words in isolation, they learn to use spelling-to-sound correspondences to help select from among a few possible alternatives. Very few of all these aspects of reading are expressly taught. How, then, does anyone ever learn to read?

SUMMARY

There are many different kinds of text to be read and many different purposes for reading. The one aspect of reading that all have in common is that questions are asked of the text. Understanding occurs when answers to these questions are found. None of this is unnatural in any way, nor does it need to be taught. The ability to ask relevant questions and to know where to find answers in print depends on familiarity with the type of material involved and the particular purpose of the reading, both of which develop with experience in reading.

CHAPTER 2

Learning to Be a Reader

Babies strive to make sense of the world, to read and interpret its signals and signs, from the moment they are born. At first, perhaps, they are concerned only with their own well-being. How else could they survive? But soon they are exploring the constraints and possibilities that the world offers, starting with their own bodies—*What can I do with my hands, my legs, my senses, my voice? Where can I move myself without disaster? Where can I find support? What does everything going on around me mean?*

Infants quickly begin to interpret the behavior of others—*Does this mean I'm going to be fed, bathed, taken out, or settled down to sleep? Is anyone paying attention to me? What is everyone up to?* None of this is *explained* to infants; they have to read the signs for themselves. Not only must they interpret, they must reflect upon whether they've been right or wrong. They demonstrate that they can recognize their own successes and failures of interpretation, and learn.

Soon infants are paying particular attention to certain structured noises emitted from the mouths of people around them—*Are these deliberately contrived sounds to be ignored or interpreted? Do they have meaning, in the same way that facial expressions and bodily gestures have meaning?* And skillfully and selectively, infants begin to read meaning into the noises that people make. They begin to interpret, understand, and use speech, the *auditory* form of language.

They also quickly begin to interpret visual signs and symbols in the world around them, whenever they see something that appears to be put there for a purpose, such as the eye-catching logos and trademarks that festoon our streets, malls, and television screens. Children are not so much interested in how something *looks* as in what it *means* to them. They begin to pay attention to the *visible* form of language, as soon as they realize that the marks convey a meaning.

With all this inquiry and interpretation going on from birth, I don't think it comes as a great surprise to children to discover that there are visual characteristics of the world that have just as much structure and meaning, or potential meaning, as speech—especially if they have had the good fortune of being read to, whether entire books or mere fragments of written language like names, signs, and labels. Once children grasp that written language can be full of meaning—useful, relevant, reassuring, and engrossing—there's usually no stopping them.

Making sense of print can only get difficult when someone breaks the meaningful flow of spoken and written language into meaningless fragments, like "that's a *b* . . . " and even worse "*b* is pronounced *buh.*" Their reading of this kind of situation is likely to tell children that they are confronted by nonsense, which every fiber of their mind tells them should be ignored.

But that is getting ahead of the story. Before discussing why so much of what is called "literacy instruction" is nonsensical, we should look in more detail at why reading—in the more specific sense of interpreting the symbols of written language—should have the potential of making so much sense, and of being essentially comprehensible and learnable, in the first place.

NO MAGICAL MOMENT

The phrase *learning to read* can be misleading if it is taken to mean that there is a magical day in every literate person's life, some kind of a threshold, on which we became a reader but before which we couldn't read at all. We begin learning to read the first time we make any kind of sense of print, even just a one-word sign, and we learn something about reading every time we read.

On the other hand, there's very little we can learn about reading without reading, and in this context I'm referring specifically to reading written words in settings in which they make sense. I'm not referring to drills and exercises with letters, syllables, nonsense words, or even words when they are in sequences and situations that serve no purpose and make no sense. Children don't need nonsense in order to learn to read; they need to read. Let me repeat: *to learn to read, learners need to read.*

The notion that learning to read is somehow different from reading, and antecedent to it, becomes particularly dangerous with older students experiencing difficulty with reading (or diagnosed as having difficulty), who may be restricted to activities that make no sense to them in order that they can "acquire basic skills." But the truly basic skills of reading, discussed throughout this book, can never be taught directly and are only accessible to learners through the experience of reading. Not only does meaningful reading provide the essential clues and feedback for learning to read, it provides its own rewards. Becoming a reader is a satisfying activity. What encourages children to read, and thus to learn to read, isn't some promise of satisfaction in the future, or an "extrinsic reward" like praise, high marks, a special treat, or the avoidance of derision or punishment, but being able to read. Watch children engrossed in a book from which they are learning about reading, and there will be no need to ask where the fundamental satisfaction lies.

THE ROOTS OF READING

How do children begin reading? "Learning to read by reading" may seem to presuppose that there is already some reading ability as a basis for further learning. But how does reading get started?

There are two questions, one theoretical and the other practical. The theoretical question is: Where do the roots of reading lie; what are the basic insights that children need in order to begin to read? The practical question is: How can children develop reading ability before they know sufficient words to read any book? There is a simple answer to the practical question, so I shall mention it briefly and then postpone the detailed discussion for a while. If children can't read well enough to learn to read by reading, then someone else has to do their reading for them. The other question is far more basic and important, though it is asked less often: Where do the roots of reading lie? That is the question I want to deal with first.

Two fundamental insights are required before any child can begin to learn to read, although these first steps in reading are almost invariably overlooked in discussions of how reading should be taught. They are the insights that (1) *written language makes sense* and that (2) *written language is different from speech*.

Insight 1: Written Language Makes Sense

It is obvious that children must be able to distinguish written words from each other. They must learn that one arrangement of printed marks indicate the word (or rather the meaning) *horse* while another arrangement indicates *cow*, and so forth. In itself, this learning requirement shouldn't be a great problem. Learning to recognize individual words goes on through life—at least 50,000 times for a moderately experienced reader. But underlying this very general ability is a fundamental insight that each reader must achieve once, but only once. This insight is that the visible marks that are written language are meaningful, they make sense, and there is some point in distinguishing them from each other. Print isn't arbitrary, like the pattern of the wallpaper or the decoration around the label on a package; different patterns of print must be treated differently. The differences are significant.

We take it for granted when we tell children that a certain pattern of marks on paper says their name, or that another is the word *dog*, that they understand what we are talking about and have intuited that print has a meaningful function. But until the realization clicks that printed marks are distinguishable from each other in ways that make a difference, that they have a use, reading can't begin. I'm not sure how all children first get this essential insight, but I can give an example of one child who had just achieved it.

Matthew, 3 years old and certainly not a reader by most criteria, could recognize only a few words (his name and one or two words in favorite picture books) and hadn't yet mastered all the letters of the alphabet. But in a department store he knew how people located the section that sold greeting cards. He pointed to a sign hanging over the greeting card counter and correctly explained, "That sign says *cards*." How did he know? It wouldn't be particularly interesting if Matthew had been able to identify the word because his parents had "taught" it to him; that wouldn't demonstrate that he understood the function of words. He might merely have learned to parrot a response to a particular printed mark, just as he might have learned quite meaninglessly to call a certain object a "dictionary" without having any understanding of what a dictionary is. But in another department Matthew was confronted by a word that was certainly unfamiliar. He took one look at the word *luggage*, glanced around him, and said that the word must be "cases." Here in this "error" was the clue that Matthew had the insight that print has meaning. He was able to impose a meaning on a word—to predict a meaning for it—even though he wasn't able to recognize that particular word. It is the same with a child who makes a squiggle with a crayon on a sheet of paper and asks us to read it.

Every reader needs the insight that the printed words in a book are meaningful—they are language—and can be interpreted in terms of a story or useful information. We hear a lot about the importance of a literate home, of growing up in an environment of books and other reading material, but what exactly does a child learn from such surroundings? Reading isn't "caught" from exposure to print, like an infection. What sense does a child make out of it? To say that a child hears an adult reading a story and therefore understands that the adult is getting the words from the text is an incomplete explanation at best. Many adults understand that music comes from the speakers of a stereo system without understanding exactly how the sounds they hear are related to the surface of the spinning disk. How is a child to know that putting a book into the hands of an adult doesn't generate or inspire the sounds of reading aloud in the same way that putting a disk into a slot makes the sounds of music? Of course, from our superior position of knowing how to read, we think it ludicrous—if we think about it at all—that reading might be a complete mystery to a child, something more akin to a ritual than a skill. But we are looking at the situation from a very favored position. Like many experts, we find it difficult to adopt the perspective of beginners who can't see what is so obvious to us.

Insight 2: Written Language Is Different from Speech

It is difficult to understand anything in a language that we aren't familiar with, whether written or spoken. I'm not talking about foreign languages here, but about different ways of putting words of a familiar language together—different jargons, idioms, or "manners of speaking."

It is usually obvious that written language is not the same as speech. You can generally tell if a person is reading a speech or talking spontaneously, just as you can generally tell if an article has been written or is an unedited transcript of a speech. There are differences in vocabulary, grammar, sentence organization, complexity, and formality.

There is nothing unusual about these differences between writing and speech; spoken language varies considerably from occasion to occasion, for every speaker. It's a mistake to talk about "spoken language" as if it were just one invariable way of talking. People talk differently, depending on whom they are talking to, what they are talking about, and the circumstances in which they are talking. Even children know about this, and they are highly sensitive to people who talk to them in unconventional or inappropriate ways. These different ways of talking are known technically as *registers*, and one of the crucial skills of being able to talk is to understand and employ appropriate registers. Unfamiliarity with a register—for example, the "academic register" of many school situations—is one of the reasons children with perfectly adequate language abilities in situations with which they are familiar can appear to have very little ability to speak or comprehend in school.

The multiple registers of spoken language are not defects—they aren't degraded versions of "proper English." They have a communicative function—balancing the demands put on speakers to be comprehensible and precise with the needs of listeners to find and select the information they need to comprehend. But the registers also have a social role, establishing that participants are observing expected interpersonal conventions and that they are "on the same wavelength." New registers recognizing both communicative and interpersonal imperatives are well established in the electronic exchanges of the Internet.

Written language also differs from speech for the very good reason that the relative demands put on speakers and listeners are not the same as the demands put on writers and readers. Therefore written language is different. In fact, there are many different registers of written language—the language of children's stories is not the same as the language of newspapers or magazines, which is not the same as the language of personal correspondence, of interdepartmental memoranda, or of advertisements. And we think it odd, if not wrong, when registers are confused.

The differences among registers of language are important because it is always difficult to understand a language we're unfamiliar with, especially if we fail to find the emotional and empathetic tone we are often looking for.

How do inexperienced readers become familiar with the registers of written language? I've already indicated the obvious solution: Someone has to read to them until they can read for themselves. A major advantage for children who have the opportunity to listen to stories is that they become used to the language employed in them and don't find stories strange when they begin to read for themselves.

INSIGHTS RELATED TO INSTRUCTION

There are two other insights that aren't essential for learning to read but that become important if learners are to make sense of a good deal of reading instruction. Some methods of instruction take these insights for granted, although they are extremely difficult to achieve before learners become readers of some experience.

The first instructional insight is that written words (in English and some other languages) can be broken down into smaller units called letters that have a relation to spoken language. Many children find this a difficult concept because individual letters don't "make sense" in the way that a whole word can be meaningful. No one can point to a "kay" or an "ell" or a "doubleyou" as something meaningful in the world around us. One 6-year-old who knew quite a lot about reading complained as she struggled with the printed word *dog* under a picture of a dog: "I know this word is *dog*, and I could read it even if the picture wasn't there, but I don't understand what I'm supposed to do with this 'dee' and 'o' and 'gee' the teacher keeps talking about." The insight that there is a relationship between written and spoken language—a very tenuous one—can wait until after reading begins (as illustrated by Matthew a few paragraphs ago) and should come without difficulty as new readers gain experience.

Another set of insights demanded by particular forms of instruction rather than by the essential nature of reading is related to special terms such as *letter*, *word*, and *sentence*. These words tend to be used with great abandon in instruction, and anyone who can read takes them for granted as simple and obvious terms. But many children have difficulty understanding them, because terms like *word*, *letter*, and *sentence* aren't easily related to spoken language. They are primarily terms that relate to written language and therefore only make sense when you can read.

Certainly there is nothing like a "letter" in spoken language. When we comprehend spoken language, we don't break it down into separate sounds like "duh-oh-guh is *dog*," even though speech is often discussed in that way in reading instruction. Nor does speech consist of words in any conspicuous manner. Even in formal registers, spoken words are run together. It is difficult to know where one word ends and the next begins (unless you already know what the words are, of course). We don't break up the elements of speech into—separate—units—like—this. A word as a distinct unit is something that exists primarily in written language, something with a space on either side, or in a dictionary. And who ever talks about a "sentence" in normal speech? The only person who might say "Listen to my sentence" rather than "Listen to what I'm saying" is the judge at a trial. In fact, it is impossible to say what a sentence is without referring to aspects of written language, like capital letters and punctuation.

The ability to employ specialized terms like *letter*, *word*, and *sentence* is sometimes referred to as "reading readiness" (and even by ominous expressions like "metalinguistic awareness"), but it has nothing to do with reading. Many children learn to read without understanding what these terms mean, just as they learn to talk before comprehending (if ever) such specialized grammatical expressions as *noun*, *verb*, and *adjective*. But if a teacher makes it necessary for children to understand terms like *letter*, *word*, *syllable*, and *paragraph*—or to detect isolated "sounds" in spoken language (referred to as "phonemic awareness")—then obviously children who can't do these things will have trouble in making sense of the instruction, let alone in learning to read. Difficulty in particular kinds of instruction doesn't mean that a child is not ready to learn to read; it simply underlines that aspects of instruction can be inappropriate, confusing, and unnecessary.

MAKING SENSE OF LEARNING TO READ

Clearly, reading has many facets that must be mastered in a variety of different situations. Nevertheless, there is one general answer to the question of how children learn to read, and that is *by making sense of written language*. A corollary to this statement is that children don't learn to read from instruction or from material that is nonsense to them.

Children don't learn to read in order to make sense of print. They strive to make sense of print and as a consequence learn to read. The sequence of events is identical with the way in which spoken language is learned. Children don't learn to talk in order to communicate and to make sense of the language that they hear. As they make sense of language spoken around them, they learn to understand speech and to employ it themselves, to complement other means of communication they already command.

There is nothing remarkable about this phenomenon of comprehension preceding competence. In fact, understanding that children's first efforts are always to make sense of the world removes much of the mystery from how they come to master spoken and written language.

Children would never learn to talk if they waited for us to teach them speech the way we often try to teach them to read, one trivial bit of information after another. But children strive to make sense of the environment they are in, provided the environment has the possibility of making sense. Children can make sense of spoken and written language in the way that they make sense of everything else in their world. They are only confounded by nonsense.

We tend to overlook that the majority of children grow up in a world in which they are surrounded by print, almost all of it meaningful, just as they develop spoken language in environments where they are immersed in meaningful spoken language. Books are important, but it is a mistake to equate the written language environment of children with the number of books they see in their homes. Children don't need the supposed advantage of "literate" parents—unless it is falsely assumed that children who don't come from "literate" backgrounds will somehow be incapable of learning to read.

Try to look at the world through a child's eyes. As you stroll through a shopping mall you are bombarded by print from all sides and from above—product labels, packages, prices, posters, slogans, lists, directions, greeting cards, magazines, wrappers—much of which repeats print found in the home or seen on television or on computer monitors. As adults, we tend to pay little conscious attention to all this print for the simple reason that it is so familiar to us. We take it for granted. But to a child the print is a constant challenge, a persistent problem, something that must and can be made sense of.

Few children are completely unaware of telephone directories and catalogs, of magazines and newspapers with their sports pages, entertainment guides, and comic strips. Along the street there are traffic signs, storefronts, advertising, menus, mailboxes, posters, billboards, and doors labeled with very significant print. Practically every appliance and piece of equipment bears a manufacturer's name and significant words like *fuel, lights,* or *on* and *off.* And just about all of this ocean of print is meaningful, it makes a difference. When the word STOP occurs in the real world, it is not a pointless series of squiggles with no relation to anything else around. It is not there for people to read aloud, to decode into spoken language, to bark "st-o-puh, *stop*" at each other. The written word STOP means "Here's where you have to stop, right now." It makes sense. It is there for a reason.

Think of the print on television—not only the representations of people reading in so many aspects of daily life, but the written language that is part of every commercial. The text of many television commercials is among the most informative written language that children can see, since at the same time that words are presented visually—the product name and perhaps some words like *new! improved!*—they are often also spoken aloud and accompanied by a picture that demonstrates the meaning of the message.

A child is surrounded by written language and learns about reading by making sense of it, solving such problems as "Why is it there?" and "What does it signify?" Children must discover the different ways in which various examples of print have to be interpreted and remember how to distinguish one form from another in the future. But these problems are no different in essence from learning how to distinguish one thing from another, which children of preschool age solve with ease thousands of times.

Written language presents problems, but in the real world it also contains the clues to their solution. Every meaningful piece of print not only helps children gain the general insights they need about the nature and functions of written language, but also offers specific hints about the likely meanings of particular words. Because print in the real world is so often meaningful, it also provides the test for the solutions that children hypothesize. Children quickly discover whether they have correctly read the words *closed, no exit, toys, gum,* or *restroom.*

Not that adults have nothing to do with all this learning. The critical role that adults play in helping children in this fundamental task of making sense of print is to make sense of print for them. Just as adults unwittingly make it possible for children to learn spoken language by talking to them (and around them) in situations that make sense to the children, so adults can help children master print by the simple practice of reading to them the print to which their attention is drawn. All of the specialized aspects of reading—like using telephone directories, consulting menus, comparing catalogs—are learned through models and guidance contributed by people who know how to do these things. It's not so much a matter of teaching these skills to children as doing them alongside children, showing how and why the act is performed.

When children need to know something about print or when their attention can be drawn to print—on a package, on a street sign, in an advertisement—there is an opportunity for an adult to help them learn to read by doing the reading for them. Anything in the world of print surrounding children can be read to them with profit. Telling children what a written word says won't solve their problems for them, but the assistance provides children with the opportunity to solve problems for themselves. And they will solve the problem of distinguishing words in the same way that they solve the problem of distinguishing for everything else—by looking for and testing hypotheses about significant differences.

Of course, it doesn't hurt for a child to have some acquaintance with the alphabet. For an adult to say, "See how these two words both begin with the letter B" might be helpful in drawing a child's attention to distinctive aspects of print. But learning the alphabet is not a prerequisite for learning to distinguish words, and the alphabet can be a handicap if adults try to use it to train children to sound out words before they are able to make sense of what the adults are talking about. Being able to recognize words makes sense of learning letters.

It is an excellent idea for children to have stories read to them, but initially at least, the isolated but meaningful words and fragments of sentences that children naturally meet in the world of print around them are probably as important in getting them started in reading as formal sessions around a book. Reading stories to children has two general advantages, however. The first is that the insight that interesting stories come from the printed marks in books can have a highly motivating effect on children, provided, of course, that the stories are genuinely interesting and aren't forced on beginners. The second advantage of reading to children is that it acquaints them with the peculiarities and conventions of written language registers. Children need to become acquainted with the language of books; it isn't the language they hear spoken around them in their daily life, and it is unrealistic to expect them to learn this unfamiliar style at the same time that they learn to read.

One distinctive aspect of the written language of stories is that its meaning is usually completely removed from any kind of external support or verification. If children don't understand what somebody says to them in the home or on the street, they can usually get clues to the meaning from the general situation, and even from facial expressions and other gestures. But doubt about written language has to be resolved from within the text itself (except sometimes for limited clues provided by illustrations), and experience is required to develop the habit of using the thread of an argument or story as a clue to the meaning of language. Children can acquire this experience by having written language read to them.

There is no need for concern that children who have the words on candy wrappers or the text of schoolbooks read to them will become lazy and reluctant to read for themselves. Children allow adults or other children to read for them for just as long and as much as they are unable to read themselves. As they develop competence in reading, they will take over from a person reading for them. Their impatience soon shows when they are forced to listen to something they can read for themselves.

SUMMARY

To learn to read, children must see ways of employing reading to further their own aims and interests. If written language is made meaningful to them, they will learn in exactly the same way that they learn about spoken language. Children need others to read to them, and for them, until they can read for themselves. Stories are important and helpful—especially because children learn a great deal about reading from authors—but so too are signs, labels, and the other instances of working print in the environment.

CHAPTER 3

The Limitations of Phonics

My preference at this point would be to continue the narrative into some crucial and interesting aspects of reading, such as the strictly limited role of the eyes, the importance of memory, the heart of meaning, and the nature of language and thought generally. But I must digress into a topic that intrudes into every discussion of reading, and into classrooms as well, often with a good deal of political, bureaucratic, and authoritative weight behind it. I refer to the topic of *phonics*, an instructional methodology based on the widespread misconception that reading requires the "decoding" of written language into spoken language by "sounding out" the letters of the alphabet so that print is transformed into speech. In this view, reading is accomplished by hearing sounds that you make to yourself when looking at print.

I have explained how children make sense of written language in exactly the same way they make sense of any other aspect of their visual experience, by relating what they see to its meaning, to the function it seems to fulfill in the world. I have also described briefly how children learn to read, usually by someone else helping them to make sense of written language until they are able to begin reading themselves.

But this is not the way reading is frequently taught. Many people, in school and out, believe that reading is a matter of "decoding" written language to speech, so that sense is made of spoken language, not written. The common practice, urged these days by many official, expert, and commercial sources, is for children to learn the sounds of all the individual letters, the system known as *phonics*. Unfortunately, however, individual letters, with rare and obvious exceptions, do not have any meaning until they become parts of words, so trying to teach children to read by teaching them the sounds of letters is literally a meaningless activity.

In the face of such widespread misunderstanding, the present chapter may appear negative and discouraging. But from then on, everything will be positive, encouraging, and supportive. You will have, I hope, a better understanding of why everything can often go so well and so smoothly as children learn to read, but why with inappropriate instructional techniques, things can frequently seem confusing and pointless to the learner.

THE DECODING POINT OF VIEW

What might be called the official point of view about reading is that it is simply a matter of "decoding to sound," of translating the letters of written language into the sounds of speech. Meaning is then assumed to be instantly available in the sounds of speech that the reader imagines hearing, just as it would be apparent if the reader were actually listening to someone else reading aloud. But meaning is not immediately available in either written or spoken utterances. Like everything else in the world, speech has to be interpreted. Even if readers were able to decode written language into speech, they would still be confronted by the problem of trying to determine meaning from what has now become spoken language.

In any case, it's not possible to decode written language into speech, at least not without first comprehending the written language. And if written language must be comprehended before being decoded into speech, then of course it's not necessary to decode into speech at all. We can read—in the sense of understanding print—without producing or imagining sounds.

The argument that writing can't be translated into speech without prior understanding undermines one of the most hallowed educational dogmas—that the way to teach reading is to teach phonics, or spelling-to-sound correspondence rules. But as a means of "decoding" written language into speech, phonics just doesn't work. To expect readers, especially beginners, to learn and rely upon phonics is to distract them with involved and unreliable procedures that are in fact largely unnecessary. Not only does the development of fluency in reading demand very little in the way of prior knowledge of spelling-to-sound correspondences, but the practice of reading itself provides the implicit understanding of those correspondences that readers require.

If we examine first the nature of the relationship between letters and sounds, we shall be in a better position to see that rather than phonics making reading possible, it is reading that makes phonics seem to work. If it seems obvious that the sounds of the letters C-A-T can be put together to make the spoken word *cat*, that is because we have learned, through reading, that the written word CAT is pronounced "cat." We have learned to pronounce the word, not the letters. In the process of examining phonics as an instructional method—and there are many different views on how phonics should be taught—we may see how it is that many children are able to learn to read despite the phonics instruction they receive.

THE PHONICS FALLACY

The issue concerns the number and nature of the relationships, or correspondences, between the letters of written language and the sounds of speech. There would be a perfect one-to-one correspondence between the two aspects of language if every letter stood for just one sound and every sound was represented by just one letter. Then indeed it might be of some use to children to learn the rules of spelling-to-sound correspondence. In the same mechanical way computers could also be programmed to convert written language into speech. All that would be needed is a set of spelling-to-sound rules to connect individual letters that can be "recognized" by the optical systems employed by computers to devices for synthesizing the sounds of speech. But the reason phonics doesn't work for children or for computers is that the relationships between the letters and sounds can't be uniquely specified. Human readers and computers must have entire words—and much more besides—in their memory before they can recognize words, which makes individual spelling-to-sound correspondences largely redundant. The problem is not that the correspondences aren't known, but that they are too complex. They are not one-to-one.

For a start, our written language is provided with an alphabet of just 26 letters, while there are about 40 distinctive sounds in spoken English. Obviously some letters must correspond to more than one sound. In fact, there is not one letter in our alphabet that isn't associated with more than one sound, like the C in *carry* and the C in *city* (or with silence, like the first C in *science*). Nor is there any single sound of speech that is represented by only one letter. Spelling-to-sound correspondences are not one-to-one, but many-to-many. And there lies the core of the problem of phonics for human readers and for computers: to know which of the many-to-many correspondences should apply on a particular occasion. There may be half a dozen alternative ways of pronouncing individual letters and no reliable phonic guide as to when each of the alternatives applies.

The sequence of letters C-A-T, for example, could be pronounced *such*, according to phonics rules. C is often pronounced /s/, as in *city*; the letter A can be pronounced /uh/, as in *about*, and T can be pronounced /ch/ as in *picture*. Of course it seems absurd to suggest that C-A-T might be decoded to *such*, but that is because we learned to read the word *cat* as a whole. We don't see anything absurd about the pronunciation of C, A, and T in *city*, *about*, and *picture*. Even phonics would say that different rules apply in these cases. Once I begin to explain this, it will be seen why phonics is so complicated, confusing, and of minimal utility.

RULES AND EXCEPTIONS

Some simplification can be achieved by recognizing that we cheat with the alphabet and use it as if there were in fact more than 26 letters. This expansion is achieved by employing combinations of letters to represent sounds that are certainly not combinations of sounds corresponding to the letters considered independently. For example, the various sounds we give to the letter combination TH—like the sounds at the beginning of *thin* and *this*—are in no way blends of any possible sounds of T and H considered separately. Some alphabets are a little more straightforward about such matters. Greek, for example, has the single character "theta" (θ) for the initial sound in *thin*, which English represents by a two-letter combination, and another character "delta" (δ) for the same English combination TH at the beginning of words like *this*. In the same way, the Greek alphabet has the character "phi" (φ) for the sound we represent by the two letters PH at the beginning of *phonics*. But then English also has the single letter F for the same purpose.

Because of the tendency of English to use combinations of letters for sounds that can't be considered combinations of single letter sounds, linguists prefer not to regard the 26 letters of the alphabet alone as the basic elements of written language. They talk instead of a larger set of spelling units that include all 26 single letters and a number of combinations of letters as well. Many combinations of vowels are regarded as spelling units because, like consonant combinations such as PH, TH, and SH, they behave differently when they are together than they do when they are by themselves. The vowel sound in the middle of the word *coat*, for example, can't be regarded as a combination of the vowel sounds in the words *cot* and *cat*, any more than the vowel sound in the middle of *coot* can be regarded as two occurrences of the sound in the middle of *cot*.

At first glance, the idea of treating combinations of letters as basic units of written language, with spelling-to-sound correspondences of their own, might appear to be nothing but advantageous. Certainly, the more letters that are taken into account at one time, the fewer correspondences there are likely to be. The letter O, when considered by itself, can be involved in about a dozen different pronunciations, but for the spelling unit OO there are only three corresponding sounds (as in *brook*, *broom*, and *blood*) while the combinations OOK and OOM (but not OOD) have only one. TH has two pronunciations, but THR only one. However, the argument that spelling-to-sound correspondences become simpler as the sequences of letters considered as single units become longer demands some restraint; otherwise one finishes up asserting that readers need to consider whole words as a unit before trying to pronounce them, which demolishes the rationale for using phonics in the first place. Even at the level of entire words, there is not always a one-to-one correspondence. Some words (like *read*, *lead*, *wind*, and *wound*) have different pronunciations for the same spelling, while other words have different spellings for the same pronunciation (like *so*, *sow*, and *sew*; or *their* and *there*).

Moreover, another insoluble problem for human readers and for computers expected to identify words on the basis of phonics alone is having to decide whether certain combinations of letters should be treated as spelling units or not. There are no phonic rules to indicate whether TH should be regarded as a single unit, as in *father*, or as two separate letters, as in *fathead*. How can the different functions of PH be distinguished in *elephant*, *haphazard*, or *shepherd*, or SH in *bishop* and *mishap*?

Because decisions about what constitutes a spelling unit of English are arbitrary, estimates of the number of spelling units that written

English contains vary widely among theorists, from fewer than 50 to more than 70. One might think that with about 50 spelling units in written language and 40 sounds of speech, a one-to-one correspondence between the basic units of writing and speech might come closer. But such is not the case. An exact figure can't be given for the number of correspondences that have been identified between spellings and sounds in English because the number of correspondences goes up with the number of words examined. An analysis of 20,000 common English words revealed a total of over 300 correspondences.

This total can't be reduced very much by cutting down on the number of words, especially as it is the common words of our language that contribute most of the complexity—such words as *the, of, was, their, money, horse,* and *enough.* Over 200 correspondences were discovered in an analysis restricted to only 6,000 of the commonest words, namely all the words of one or two syllables occurring in a survey of the spoken language of 6- to 9-year-old children. (Another 3,000 words in the survey of three syllables or more in length were ignored because they were too complicated for the analysis, though obviously not too complicated for the children to understand.) Nevertheless, in the 6,000 items that were the shortest and simplest words in the everyday language of these children, the researchers still found no fewer than 211 different correspondences. Eighty-three of these correspondences involve consonants, which are generally thought to be relatively straightforward; 79 involve just the six vowels when they occur alone (A, E, I, O, U, or Y); and the remaining 49 involve combinations of vowels.

There we have a measure of the complexity of the spelling-to-sound correspondences of our language, the system that phonics aims to teach in the form of "rules" for decoding writing to sound. Not only is the system massive and complex, it is also unreliable, because it contains no way of predicting when a particular correspondence applies. What is the use of a complex set of rules if there is no reliable guide for when a particular rule should be employed? What use are they to a learner?

It might be argued that many of the 211 correspondences should not be regarded as rules but rather as "exceptions." But such a distinction plays with words. One could argue that only 20 of the 211 correspondences should be considered rules and that the other 191 correspondences are exceptions. But then the burden of remembering the exceptions would be greater than the economy of remembering the rules. Alternatively, it could be argued that only 10 or so of the correspondences are exceptions, but then there will be about 200 rules. The researchers who analyzed the 211 correspondences in the 6,000 words used by children made the quite arbitrary decision that 166 of these correspondences should be regarded as rules and 45 as exceptions—and then found that their decision made exceptions of more than 600 of the commonest words in the language.

Furthermore, there is no rule that will tell a child whether a word should be regarded as an exception or not. Where is the sense in remembering a lot of rules if you have to recognize a word before you can tell whether it follows the rules or not?

It doesn't help to say that phonics may not be perfect but it gives a reasonable idea of how a word is likely to sound. A rather generous estimate gives correspondence rules, on the average, a chance of being right three times out of four. But the chance is with one sound. The average word has at least four sounds in it, and a 1-in-4 possibility of error on single sounds goes up to 3-in-4 over sequences of four sounds. The appropriate pronunciation will be produced only 25 percent of the time. This is the fallacy underlying phonics: the belief that there actually could be a set of rules that work efficiently to decode written language into sound. Even computers can't do this, and they can be programmed with almost anything. The computers that appear able to read aloud don't rely on phonics. They depend on being able to recognize whole words, and even then they need additional information about the grammatical role and meaningful function of many words in order to achieve reasonably comprehensible pronunciation.

I'm not exaggerating. The spelling-to-sound correspondences of English are so confusing that in my judgment children who believe they can read unfamiliar words just by "blending" or "sounding them out" are likely to develop into disabled readers. They may be condemned for being "functionally illiterate" because they do exactly what they have been taught and try to read by putting together the sounds of letters.

Besides, I think it would be difficult to exaggerate the complexity and unreliability of phonics. To take just one very simple example, how are the letters HO pronounced? Not in a trick situation, as in the middle of a word like *shop,* but when H and O are the first two letters of a word. Here are 11 common words in each of which the initial HO has a different pronunciation: *hot, hope, hook, hoot, house, hoist, horse, horizon, honey, hour, honest.* Can anyone really believe that a child could identify these words by sounding out the letters?

Incidentally, although children are taught always to read from left to right, the preceding illustration shows that phonics requires reading from right to left. The 11 different pronunciations of HO that I have just given all depend on the letters that come next. The pronunciation of G or P or K at the beginning of a word depends on whether the second letter is N. The right-to-left principle has very few exceptions—*ash* and *wash, blood* and *mood, host* and *ghost.* The principle is observed, though never acknowledged, in one of the first phonics rules taught at school that vowels in the middle of a word "say their name" if the word ends with "silent e," as in *hat* and *hate, mop* and *mope.*

MAKING PHONICS WORK

How then can one account for the wide appeal of phonics? One explanation must be that many people simply think that phonics should work. After all, words are made up of letters, and what are letters for if readers are going to ignore them? I shall reply to that argument in the section on spelling a little later in this chapter. But first I want to show that phonics gets credit that it doesn't deserve. There is in fact a rule that ensures that phonics works. The rule is very simple: *Phonics works if you know what a word is likely to be in the first place.* Everything else encourages guesswork, which is often reckless.

I'm not being facetious. Once you recognize a word as *hotel,* you don't need to wonder about the other 10 pronunciations of HO that are possible; in fact, it probably won't occur to you to think of them. You're not likely to consider all the different ways a word might be pronounced if you already know how it is pronounced. Therefore phonics always looks obvious to people who can read. It's not surprising that children who are best at phonics are the best readers—they have to be. A cynic (or realist) has said that the smart children keep one phonics lesson ahead of the teacher—and the smart teacher keeps one phonics lesson behind the children.

The fact that you need to know what a word might be in order to make sense of phonics is employed in some of the more sophisticated attempts to develop rules for transforming written language to sound. Some linguists, for example, recognize that spelling-to-sound correspondence rules are easier to apply if the meaning of words is taken into account. They point out that the different role of TH in *father* and in *fathead* is easy to detect if it is taken into account that *father* is one distinct word and *fathead* is two. Put another way, phonics works if you understand the word in the first place. The researchers working on the 211 correspondences described above devised a simple rule for distinguishing the short /a/ at the beginning of words like *about, adore,* and *ago* from the long /a/ at the beginning of words like *able, acorn,* and *apron.* Since all these are words of two syllables, the first consisting of just the single letter A, it might be thought that there is no way of distinguishing among them. But there is a rule; it depends on how the word is stressed. If the emphasis is on the first syllable, as in *able,* the /a/ is long; if the word is stressed on the second syllable, as in *about,* the /a/ is short. So the researchers in all seriousness included "intonation rules" in their phonics program. In plain English, if you want to know how a word is pronounced, say it.

Phonics will in fact prove of use—provided you have a rough idea of what a word is. If you know that the word you are looking at is probably *horse, cow,* or *donkey,* phonics will enable you to tell the difference. But here you don't have to run through all 11 alternatives for the first two letters of *horse,* you just have to know that a word beginning with HO couldn't be *cow* or *donkey.* And you certainly don't have to work your way through the entire word, blending all the possible combinations of sounds.

Of course, to be able to make some reasonable prediction about what a word might be, you need to be able to make sense of what you are reading. Here is another reason why learning to read is so difficult if it involves something that makes no sense to you. How can you tell what a word might be if you have no understanding of what you are reading?

The *horse, cow,* or *donkey* illustration indicates the limit to which phonics is useful, and it never requires an intensive course of phonics exercises and drills before reading begins. It is only through meaningful reading experience that the advantages and limitations of phonics make sense—and then they reveal themselves.

READING WITHOUT PHONICS

A last-ditch defense of phonics in the face of the analysis I have just presented runs like this: How is it that people are, in fact, able to read if the spelling-to-sound correspondences of our language are really so cumbersome and unpredictable? This kind of circular argument begins with the assumption that reading needs phonics and takes the fact that reading is possible as proof that phonics must work. To counter such an argument, it must be shown not only that phonics is ineffective but also that phonics is unnecessary. It must be shown that readers can recognize words and comprehend text without decoding to sound at all.

How is it possible to recognize written words without sounding them out? The answer is that we recognize words in the same way that we recognize all the other familiar objects in our visual world—trees, animals, cars, houses, cutlery, crockery, furniture, and faces—that is, "on sight." We can recognize the thousands of written words with which we are familiar for the same reason that we can recognize all the thousands of other familiar things, because we have learned what they look like. The actual process by which the visual recognition of words and objects takes place will be discussed in more detail in a later chapter, when we shall discover that there is no fundamental difference between the way we learn to recognize objects and the way we learn to recognize written words.

The fact that written words are made up of letters that seem in themselves to be related to sound is as irrelevant to their recognition as the fact that most automobiles have their model name stuck on them somewhere. Most people can distinguish one brand of car from another without having to look for the manufacturer's label. We recognize the written word *car* in the same way that we recognize a picture of a car or even a real car, by what we have learned about how the entire configuration looks. And just as we can recognize familiar cars and other objects from a glimpse of just part of the object, we can often recognize written words from a glimpse of just part of them. As I shall explain, ease of recognition depends on how much you know in advance.

It might be thought that written words look pretty much alike and that it would be harder to distinguish words like *car* and *house* than it would be to distinguish an actual car or house. But this is not the case. Researchers found that experimental viewers can more quickly say "house" when the written word is suddenly presented in front of their eyes than when they are shown a familiar picture of a house. Viewers even respond faster in reading the words *red, yellow,* or *blue* on a white sheet of paper than in saying the correct word when presented with a sheet of paper in the appropriate color.

Furthermore, it's not necessary to say what a word is to comprehend its meaning. Quite the reverse; it is often necessary to comprehend the meaning of a word before you can say what it is. In other words, meaning is directly related to the spelling of words rather than sound. How otherwise could we be aware of many spelling mistakes? The reason a teacher corrects *their* to *there* in the sentence *Go over their, please* isn't because the spelling *their* represents the wrong sound—it obviously does not—but because it represents the wrong meaning. *Pair, pare,* and *pear* all "decode" to the same sound, but each spelling has a different meaning that we recognize on sight. It is easier to understand the sentence *Eye sea too feat inn hour rheum* when you read it aloud; the sounds may be appropriate, but the spellings indicate quite different meanings. Recognizing the meaning of something, recognizing what it is, always comes before giving a name to it. We don't have to say, "There's an airplane," before we can comprehend that the object is a plane. Rather, we have to recognize what the object is before we can give it a name.

Millions of people succeed in reading languages that don't have an alphabet, where there is no possibility of reading a word unless it is recognized on sight. Languages like Chinese, for example, are ideographic. The written words are symbols for ideas, but not for specific sounds or even specific words. Thus speakers of the different Mandarin and Cantonese spoken Chinese languages, who can't understand each other's speech, can still write to one another. They both understand that a particular written symbol means "house" even though they have different spoken words for it. In the same way, English and French speakers can both understand $2 + 2 = 4$ even though one might not understand *deux et deux font quatre* and the other might not understand the English alternative. After all, we have no difficulty in attaching meaning directly to the spoken words that we know. Why should there be a unique difficulty in attaching meaning to written words? Fundamentally, there is no difference; meaning and print are related in the same manner as meaning and speech, and neither language form is subordinate to the other.

It may be objected that expecting a reader to recognize and comprehend written language directly, without first decoding to speech, would overburden memory. Isn't it unreasonable to expect children to learn to recognize and distinguish thousands of different words on sight, instead of simply memorizing a set of rules for transforming written language into speech that is already understood?

But there is no evidence that there is any limit to the capacity of human memory. The "overloading" argument mistakes the very nature of memory, regarding it as a kind of store in which items are piled up on each other, rather than as a network, a system, that can only function better with a richer interconnection of parts. If anything, adding new and meaningful elements to memory increases its efficiency.

Children memorize all the time, so effortlessly that we aren't aware that they are doing it. Only nonsense is difficult to memorize. In the first 10 years of their lives, children develop a spoken-language vocabulary that enables them to recognize and make sense of at least 20,000 words, which means an average learning rate of 2,000 words a year, more than five words a day. At the same time, children are also acquiring the knowledge that enables them to identify on sight hundreds of faces and many thousands of objects; to recall ages, birthdays, telephone numbers, addresses, and prices; to sing songs and master the rules of games; and to find their way around buildings, streets, and fields. The number of different objects we learn to distinguish and recognize is uncountable. Among such a multitude, the memorization of written words, with all the meaning that can be brought to them, is a rippling stream that loses significance as it becomes part of a broad river.

SPELLING

Why, then, have letters? If letters don't efficiently decode to sound and can trap the unwary reader into confusion and frustration, why have the dangerous things around at all? There is a simple explanation: letters are a convenience for producing written language.

Writing is much more demanding than reading, even in a narrow physical sense. Readers can flick their eyes over pages of text for hours on end without bodily fatigue, but writers must plod their way through every word, pushing their pencil or pen forward at barely a tenth of the speed that readers achieve. Even writers who employ keyboards are constrained to putting their thoughts into words at a much slower rate than the brain can comfortably produce them. Writers who dictate lose the main advantage that writers have over speakers—immediate and easy access to what they have already said.

The biggest memory problem for writers is the need to put words into visible form so that readers will be able to recognize them. A distinction must be drawn here between two different facets of memory retrieval: recognition and recall. To recognize an object, you merely have to observe that it is in some way familiar. In effect, the very object that you are looking at serves to jog your memory; often the merest glance will suffice. But recall demands reproduction of the whole thing; much more knowledge and effort are required. Think of the difference between recognizing an animal and trying to draw it. A fluent reader usually need only glance at part of the print that is on a page, but the writer has had to put all the detail in. The reader can skip but the writer can't. Chinese is no more difficult for its readers than English, although the Chinese symbols don't decode directly to sound. But writing is much harder in Chinese than in English because of the many thousands of different characters. Learning to *recognize* thousands of different forms is not such a big achievement, but learning to *reproduce* them is.

As a result, alphabets have been developed to help writers and printers remember how words should be reproduced. Thousands of complex forms have been reduced to a couple of dozen simple elements. And these elements themselves, the letters of the alphabet, are to varying degrees predictable from spoken language. Even if writers don't remember how to spell occasional words correctly, they can usually make an approximation that will tell a reader what was meant.

The mere fact that the alphabet can be employed to reduce the complex visual configurations of words into more simple elements is a help to teachers as well as to writers; it facilitates talking about how written words should look. Instead of saying, "There's a kind of goalpost at the beginning, then a big circle, and then a vertical stroke with a bar over the top," you say, "Spell it H-O-T." The simplification of thousands of complex words into a few letters made printing possible in the days when all type had to be moved by hand. The demands of the typewriter industry played a large part in the development of a phonetic alphabet for Japanese, after the failure of other attempts to fractionate words so that their parts would fit on a manageable number of keys. Similar endeavors are increasing the availability of reading materials in China, but they won't necessarily make reading any easier for the Chinese.

Readers don't *need* the alphabet (though it is useful for talking about words). For centuries people have learned to read without knowing a thing about letters, and millions still do. The Western phonetic alphabet was developed when written language moved out of the exclusive domain of the church and university, where the emphasis was on reading and interpretation, and into commerce, where every merchant wanted to write explicit records and send out unambiguous bills. It is perhaps not coincidental that the invention of alphabetic writing has been attributed to the Phoenicians, the traders of the ancient Mediterranean world.

However, writers have not been permitted to get away with a completely phonetic alphabet. The spelling of words is never a direct and unvarying representation of their sounds, and for several good reasons. First, written language is not permitted to vary with dialect (in fact, it represents no one's actual spoken language). We don't normally expect writers to reproduce words in exactly the way they hear them spoken in their part of the world or speak them themselves. A person may speak quite distinctively as a Texan or a New Englander, a Scot or an Australian, but we don't expect these idiosyncrasies to show up in the spelling of words, no matter how they charm the ear. The spelling of words is a convention that crosses hundreds of dialect boundaries. Attempts to reproduce dialect in written form do not make reading easier, even when the dialect reproduced is supposed to be our own. Written language is much more consistent than speech over time and space. The plays of Shakespeare would be much more difficult to understand today if they were written to reflect the sounds of English that Shakespeare spoke.

Another reason why spelling is not a direct reflection of the sounds of words is more fundamental. It is not basically the function of spelling to represent sound, but to represent meaning. Take some everyday examples. To change a singular written word into the plural we simply add S: *dog–dogs, cat–cats, judge–judges.* (I am ignoring the "irregular" plurals like *child–children, man–men, sheep–sheep.*) But the written S we add is an indication of meaning, of plurality, not of sound, because in speech we pluralize *dog* by adding the sound /z/ ("dogz"), *cat* by the sound /s/ ("cats"), and *judge* by the sound /iz/ ("judgiz"). Would reading be simplified if we had three general plural endings, S, Z, and IZ, that more exactly reflected sound, instead of just one? There are many other examples. The past tense of *walk* is pronounced "walkt," the past tense of *hug* is pronounced "hugd," and the past tense of *mend* is pronounced "mendid," but the single past-tense meaning that is represented by three different sounds in speech—/t/, /d/, and /id/—is represented by the single suffix ED in writing.

This tendency for spelling to remain consistent for a particular aspect of meaning despite considerable variation in sound can be summed up in a single principle: *Words that look alike tend to share meanings.* It is this principle that makes sense of the G in *sign* and *assign:* The G is not present because of any phonic rule about how the words *sign* and *assign* are pronounced, but because *sign* and *signature, assign* and *assignation* are related words—they share a common element of meaning. The "silent g" doesn't reflect an aberration of the written language but a peculiarity of speech; it is a help to the reader because of what it says about the meaning of these particular words. It might be said that the spelling of these words makes more sense than their pronunciation.

In the same way there is no need to appeal to elaborate phonic correspondences to account for the fact that the letter C sometimes has a /k/ sound, as in *medical,* and sometimes an /s/ sound, as in *medicine.* The letter C occurs in the middle of both words because it is part of the root *medic,* representing a meaning that the two words have in common. The C in the middle of *critical* and *criticize* is similarly part of a shared meaning though not a shared sound. Of course, if you try to teach children that the letters in words are supposed to stand for specific sounds, then they will see no sense in the spelling of any of the examples in this paragraph. But if the relationship between appearance and meaning is explained, then the spelling of words becomes a help rather than a hindrance, not just in the recognition of words but in their comprehension as well.

In the face of the above arguments, the efforts of many well-intentioned people to "reform" the spelling of English may be seen to lose its point. Would it really help readers to change spelling to *medisin* and *medikal?* Would it make reading (and writing) easier if people *hugd, kist,* and *congratulatid* each other? Instead of *buoy,* should some people write *boy* and others *booie,* depending on the dialect they speak? Should some people spell *caught* as *cot* but others as *court?* Does it make more sense to leave the B at the end of *bomb* or to change the spelling to *bom* and then have to explain where the B suddenly comes from in the middle of *bombard* and *bombardier?*

There is a corollary to the principle that words that look alike tend to mean alike; it is that words with different meanings tend to look different. There is no question about the differences in meaning between *their* and *there,* or among the hundreds of other pairs of words that share the same sound in speech but have different meanings that are indicated by different spellings, such as *pair, pare,* and *pear; bear* and *bare; mail* and *male; pail* and *pale; meet, mete,* and *meat;* and *so, sew,* and *sow.* Would there be any advantage in introducing additional ambiguity into written language by spelling words with different meanings in the same way?

Of course, it might be argued that a revised spelling need not be made completely dependent on sound. No system of spelling or writing reform tries to provide an exact written representation of all the sounds of speech; otherwise every different speaker would spell words in a different way. But if, in effect, you would have to learn a new dialect of spoken language simply to understand the sounds that a modified written language is supposed to decode to, then the advantage of revising written language in the first place becomes obscure. The opinion of linguists who have made an intensive study of the relationships among spelling, speech, and meaning is unequivocal: The present spelling of English offers the best system for the unambiguous representation of meaning for all the various dialects of spoken English that exist.

It is a mistake to think that the "rationalization" of spelling would help even in the teaching of reading. Such a change would be regarded as useful only by those people who maintain that the main purpose of reading is to decode letters to sounds and that comprehension is a secondary consideration.

MEETING NEW WORDS

A final defence of phonics is often this: Even if it is true that someone who knows how to read has no need to decode to sound in order to recognize familiar words, what about words that are not familiar? What happens when readers, especially beginners, encounter a word that has never before been met? Surely then there is no alternative to phonics.

But ask competent readers how they react when they meet a word they don't recognize on sight. Usually three alternative courses of action are specified, with a very definite order of preference. The first alternative and preference is to skip over the puzzling word. The second alternative is to guess what the unknown word might be. And the final and least preferred alternative is to try to sound the word out. Phonics, in other words, comes last, and with good reason, for phonics is the least efficient choice.

If you now look at children—or ask them—to discover what they do when they encounter unfamiliar words, you are likely to find a similar pattern, even for children who are struggling through their first attempts to make sense of written language. Children who are on their way to becoming readers behave in the same manner as fluent readers. Their tendency is first to skip, second to guess, third to sound out. If phonics is the first or only choice, it is because children are reflecting what they have been taught, not what helps them to read.

Skipping is by no means as inefficient or even undesirable as it might sound as a strategy for reading. Texts that are comprehensible in the first place—that aren't nonsense—remain comprehensible even if up to one word in five is completely obliterated. The identification of every word is not necessary for comprehension to take place. On the contrary, stopping to try and figure out every unfamiliar word the moment it is encountered serves only to disrupt perception and memory. Comprehension is bound to be lost in such circumstances, and learning becomes impossible. The tendency to stop dead at the first difficult word and thus to struggle uncomprehendingly through print a word at a time is a characteristic of poor readers of all ages. Even if it transpires that an unfamiliar word must be identified in order for comprehension to proceed, it is generally better to read past the difficult word and then go back. The two best clues to any word, if no help is available from any other source, are its total context—the meaning in which it is embedded—and its similarity to words that are already known.

Normally a word that is skipped is not ignored altogether. Subsequent reading usually clarifies the sense of the passage as a whole, and a grasp of the sense of the whole contributes to comprehension of words that have been left unidentified. As we shall see, this use of context to throw light on new words is the way in which most new words are learned by all readers.

Guessing has a bad reputation in education, especially among reading teachers, partly through misplaced puritanism—it may suggest that children need not apply themselves properly to their "work"—and partly because guessing is regarded as synonymous with a reckless lack of thought. But guessing, as I am using the term, is not a matter of blind, impetuous behavior, but rather the fundamental process of employing prior knowledge to eliminate unlikely alternatives. Guessing in the way I have described it is not just a preferred strategy for beginners and fluent readers alike; it is the most efficient manner in which to read and learn to read. To avoid the negative connotation, I shall refer to this precise and productive form of guessing as *prediction*.

Prediction—the elimination of unlikely alternatives—makes the third alternative for word identification possible. A knowledge of phonics will never enable children to deduce the identity of a word like *horse* (with the 11 alternative pronunciations of HO) unless they can use context to narrow the range of possibilities. The best way to work out the sound of a new word is not by trying blindly to use phonic rules but by analogy with known words of a similar spelling (or more precisely, similar appearance). Indeed, the similarity of a new word to words that are already known provides clues to both meaning and sound; it is the words that are known that make phonics seem effective with new words.

There is, however, yet another way to ascertain the identity and meaning of unfamiliar words. It is the simplest method of all, and children will make as much use of it as they are permitted. This is the method of asking someone else what a word is. Children know that the important part of learning is not finding out what a word is on the first occasion it is met—the *identification* problem—but learning how to *recognize* the same word on future occasions. Children can take care of the recognition problem if they are not handicapped in the initial identification. Identification isn't usually a difficulty, at least not before a child gets to school. Until that time an obliging adult is generally on hand who will tell a child what a word is when the child wants to know: "This word is *girl*, that word says *stop*, and that one says your name." All these words are meaningful, you will notice, at the time they are learned. The parent doesn't write "stop" on a chalkboard, stripped of all utility and relevance. The word *stop* means "stop" when it is part of a traffic sign; it is a word with a purpose, not just an empty sequence of sounds.

But at school, suddenly, the situation is likely to be reversed. The teacher may say in effect, "Good news and bad news today, children. The bad news is that no one is ever going to tell you what a written word is again. You will have to find out for yourselves. The good news is that I am going to teach you 166 phonics rules with hundreds of exceptions." Identifying words for children doesn't make them lazy; it enables them to devote more attention to the central problem of word recognition. As soon as children can use context to give them clues to new words, they quickly wean themselves from their dependence on adults, a dependence that they find time-consuming and progressively more unnecessary. It is through sense that children learn to read, and until they read well enough to make sense of what they are doing, someone must help them. Children learn to read by reading, but not all at once. They take over gradually, while other people help them at the difficult early stages. I'm not suggesting that children need to learn long lists of words or be taught words in isolation in order to read. The learning of words themselves comes easiest with meaningful reading.

It's difficult to exaggerate how much any fluent reader has learned by reading. Most people who can read have a "sight vocabulary" of at least 50,000 words; they can recognize 50,000 words on sight, in the same way that they can recognize cars and trees and familiar faces, without any sounding out. How did they learn those 50,000 words? 50,000 flashcards? Were there 50,000 occasions when they stopped to figure out a word letter by letter, sound by sound? Or even 50,000 occasions when they asked a helpful adult to identify a word? Words are learned by reading, just as speech is learned through an active involvement in spoken language. No formal exercises are required, simply the opportunity to make sense of language in meaningful circumstances.

Not only do children learn to recognize words by reading, they acquire a practical working knowledge of relevant phonics at the same time. Phonics doesn't make sense if a child must learn that the letter C sometimes has an / s / sound and sometimes a / k / sound, that it may be absorbed into a third sound in / ch / or remain silent after S. But once children can see the letter C in action in words like *medicine, medical, church,* and *scent,* they can make sense of the observation that C may have various relationships to sound. Now they can see these relationships for themselves, and start discovering further relationships as they look for similarities among written words.

Children look for relationships among words, and with good reason. As we have seen, similarities in the appearance of words give the best clues to their meaning and thus to their identification. And in the process of predicting the identity of unfamiliar words, clues based on similarities to known words combine with clues from context to permit every reader to go even further and learn the meaning of words never encountered before, in writing or in speech.

Think of all the thousands of words every adult knows—at least 50,000. We're not told the meaning of every one of these words, and it is unlikely that we have made 50,000 trips to the dictionary. We have acquired the larger part of our vocabularies by hearing words spoken in meaningful situations or by reading words written in meaningful contexts. Most people know perfectly well the meaning of a number of words that they can't pronounce—a certain indication that they acquired this meaning while reading, by a process of prediction and confirmation. If we are reading for sense, we can afford to take chances in predicting the meaning of words, for the thread of what we are reading will surely prove us right or wrong. Children do more than learn about reading when they read; they learn about language. All this will be further explored in later chapters.

SUMMARY

The system of phonics is both cumbersome and unreliable, rarely producing an accurate pronunciation for words not recognized on sight. Better ways of identifying unfamiliar words exist, such as asking someone, using clues from context, and making comparisons with known words of similar construction. Context clues, which all children use extensively in their spoken language experience, can only be employed in reading if the material makes sense. Reliance on phonics, on spelling-to-sound correspondence, is dysfunctional in fluent reading and interferes with learning to read.

CHAPTER 4

Reading—From Behind the Eyes

With the digression of phonics behind us, we can move on to some of the more interesting aspects of reading. We can begin with the fact that an essential skill of reading that no reader is ever taught is to *depend on the eyes as little as possible.*

Does the preceding statement sound absurd? I shall demonstrate that the eyes must play a relatively minor role in reading and that undue concern with the printed marks on a page serves only to make reading more difficult. It is a basic principle of vision that the more you expect the eyes to do, the less you are likely to see. This principle applies especially in reading, where too much attention to the page in front of you can have the temporary effect of making you functionally blind. The page literally becomes blank. One of the handicaps besetting children learning to read is that often they can't see more than a few letters at a time. If a teacher calls a child's attention to a particular point in a book by saying, "There are the words in front of your nose; you can see them, can't you?" it may well be that the teacher can see the words but the child can't. This impediment has nothing to do with children's eyes but rather reflects the difficulty they are having in trying to read. In fact, it is easy to put the teacher in the same visual state as the child—by making reading equally difficult for the teacher.

VISUAL AND NONVISUAL INFORMATION

Of course, the eyes have a part to play in reading. You can't read with your eyes closed (except for Braille, which is not being considered in this book), or in the dark, or if you have no printed material in front of your eyes. It is necessary for some information from print to reach your brain. Let us call this *visual information*, which obviously must be picked up by the eyes.

But visual information alone will not suffice for reading. I could allow you all the visual information available, yet still you might be unable to read. For example, I could ask you to read the following passage, which happens to be in Swedish. Unless you understand Swedish, there is no way you will be able to read it:

> Det finns inget unikt i läsningen, vare sig man ser på hjärnans
> struktur eller dess funktioner. Den medicinska vetenskapen har
> inte lokaliserat något specifikt "läscentrum" i hjärnan.

But possibly you do understand Swedish. I could still confront you with a passage of Swedish or English text that might confound your ability to read, like the following title of a seminar presentation on sea-water densities:

> Effects of differential vertical diffusivities for T and S on the time-
> dependent models of the thermohaline circulation

And finally, even if I present you with some text in a familiar language on a topic that you fully understand, it still might not be possible for you to read. For example, it could be that you haven't learned *how* to read.

I hope you will agree that in the three situations I have just described, it wouldn't be lack of visual information that prevents you from reading. There are other kinds of information that you also need, including an understanding of the relevant language, familiarity with the subject matter, and some general ability in reading. All these other kinds of information can be lumped together and called *nonvisual information*. It is easy to distinguish visual from nonvisual information. Visual information disappears when the lights go out; nonvisual information is in your head already, behind the eyes. And since both visual and nonvisual information are required for reading, their joint necessity can be represented as in Diagram 1.

TRADING TWO KINDS OF INFORMATION

It might seem that I have gone to great pains to state the obvious—that you must already have certain kinds of information in your head in order to read. But there is a relationship between visual and nonvisual information that is not so obvious but is of critical importance

Diagram 1.

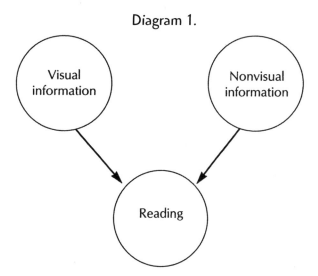

in reading: The two kinds of information can be traded off against each other. There is a reciprocal relationship between the two that might be represented as in Diagram 2 and put formally into words as follows:

> The more *nonvisual* information you have when you read, the less *visual* information you need.
> The less *nonvisual* information you have when you read, the more *visual* information you need.

Diagram 2.

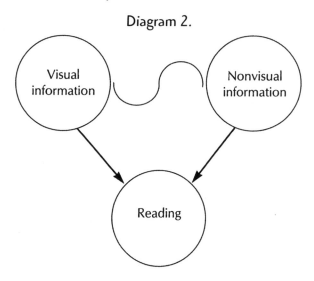

Expressed in more general terms, the more you know already, the less you need to find out. It is as if there is a certain total amount of information required to read anything (the actual amount depending on your purpose and what you are trying to read) and contributions to that total amount can come from in front of the eyes or behind.

It is easy to provide everyday illustrations of the trade-off between the two kinds of information. The more you know in advance about a book, the easier it is to read. You can read an easy book faster, you can read it in smaller print, and you can read it in a relatively poor light. A book that is difficult to read, on the other hand, requires more time, better lighting, and far more considerate printing. The eyes have more work to do if the book is difficult; often you need to peer. In the same way, it is easy to recognize billboards and highway signs from a distance when you know what the words might be, but if you have no idea or the words are in an unfamiliar language, you have to get closer to distinguish even a single letter. This is not an uncommon phenomenon; the better you are acquainted with people, or particular kinds of car, bird, or tree, the easier it is to recognize them at a distance.

The fact that visual and nonvisual information can to some extent be substituted for each other is crucial for the following reason: There is a stringent limit to how much visual information the brain can handle. The eyes can be relieved of strain in reading under less-than-ideal conditions if the reader can bring a lot of nonvisual information or prior knowledge to bear. But readers can't simply slow down and assimilate more visual information whenever the going gets tough (because there is a bottleneck between the eyes and the brain), as Diagram 3 indicates. The brain can very easily become overwhelmed by visual information, in which case the ability to see will be limited and may even cease for a while. It is therefore a basic skill of reading—a skill that can be developed only through reading—to make maximum use of what you already know and to depend on the information from the eyes as little as possible. To explain this phenomenon further, I must say a little more about the nature of seeing.

LIMITS ON SEEING

We normally assume that we can see everything that is in front of our eyes, provided of course that we have our eyes open. We also assume that vision is instantaneous, that we perceive objects and events the moment

Diagram 3.

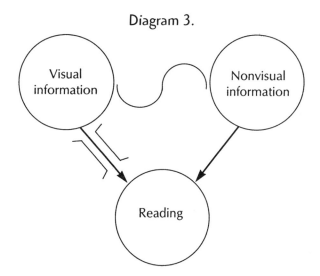

we turn our eyes to them. And we certainly tend to think that it is the eyes themselves that are responsible for what we see. But in fact the eyes don't see at all; their sole function is to pick up visual information in the form of light rays and convert it into bursts of neural energy that travel along the million or so fibers of the optic nerve into the brain. What we see is the brain's interpretation of this barrage of neural impulses.

It is the brain that sees; the eyes merely look. And the brain certainly doesn't see everything that occurs in front of the eyes. Sometimes, as everyone knows, the brain can make a mistake, in which case we can see something that isn't in front of the eyes.

Visual perception, in other words, involves decisions on the part of the brain. If you see a horse across a field, it is because the brain has decided that what you are looking at is a horse. And you will see a horse even if the brain has made a mistake and further consideration leads it to decide—and therefore see—that you are looking at a cow. If I write an address for you:

210   LION   STREET

what you see is a number, 210, and a couple of words, Lion Street. But if you check back you will see that I wrote the digits 1 and 0 in the number in exactly the same way that I wrote the letters I and O in Lion. The visual information was the same. Whether you saw numbers or letters depended on what your brain decided you were looking at.

Not only does seeing require the brain to make decisions, but the brain requires time to make these decisions. More precisely, the brain uses information—visual information—to make decisions, and the interpretation of this information takes time. The amount of time required to make a decision depends on how much information the brain needs, and the amount of information required depends basically on how many alternatives the brain has to choose among.

Even the simplest of perceptual decisions, like determining whether or not a light has flashed on, takes nearly two-tenths of a second. If the brain has to choose between two alternatives, say whether the light is red or green, the decision requires three-tenths of a second. Selecting among five alternatives requires five-tenths of a second, and among eight alternatives over six-tenths. It is true that some of this time is taken up in making a response—for example, in saying that a light of a particular color has gone on—but this response time is the same however many alternatives are involved. What makes the difference to the delay is the number of alternatives.

Of course, we aren't usually aware that we don't see everything in front of our eyes, or that a significant amount of time can elapse between looking at something and seeing it. But we are unaware because we assume we see everything instantaneously, an assumption that is itself provided by the brain. Vision, and our feelings about what we see, depend far more on the brain than on the eyes.

HOW NOT TO SEE VERY MUCH

I would like to put you into a situation in which you can get only one glance at a line of randomly selected letters, like the 25 letters in the following rectangle:

J L H Y L P A J M R W K H M Y O E Z S X P E S L M

Researchers usually contrive to limit participants in experiments to a single glance by flashing the line of letters on a screen from a slide projector or computer for about one-hundredth of a second. I can't arrange events in this book so that you will have only one glimpse of the line of letters; you are clearly free to inspect it for as long as you like. But I can ask you to use your imagination, and if you wish to check on me you can put a friend into the experimental situation by covering the rectangle with an index card. When your friend is ready, with attention focused on the center of the card, slide the card away quickly to permit a glimpse of the letters. But in the same movement bring the card back again to cover the letters once more, to prevent a second look.

The question is: How many letters can be seen in a single glance, in one brief input of visual information? Are you ready—in your imagination—for me to let you look at the letters for just a moment? There they were! How much did you see? And the answer is: not very much. You saw only four or five letters, clustered around the point where you happened to be focusing. If you were looking in the middle of the rectangle, for example, you might have been able to recognize W K H M Y. You would have seen that other letters were present, but you would not have been able to say what they were.

So now we have an answer to the question of how much can be seen in a single glance, at least as far as a line of random letters is concerned: four or five. And I must point out that this limitation has nothing to do with age, skill, or experience. One of the oldest findings in experimental psychology is that four or five letters are the upper limit on how much can be seen in the situation I have described. Children reasonably familiar with the alphabet perform almost as well on such a task as adults with many years' experience in reading, and practice will not make anyone very much better.

Nor does it make any difference how long the letters are flashed on the screen or exposed by the moving card, provided the observer gets only one glance. It isn't the rate at which visual information gets to the eye that puts the limit on how much can be seen in a single glance, but how long the brain takes to make its decisions. Information gets to the eye, and thereby becomes available to the brain, almost instantaneously. It doesn't matter whether the flash on the screen (or the movement of the card) is as brief as one-thousandth of a second, provided there is adequate illumination. In that instant, information from the display gets into the visual system. After that instant, the brain begins to work and the eyes in effect shut down (though they may stay open). The work of the eyes is done for the moment; any additional information they might pick up will serve only to overload the brain. The fact that the visual information might be available in front of the observer's eyes for a total of a fifth of a second—200 times as long as the minimum exposure required—will make absolutely no difference. Nothing more will be seen. The brain is too busy trying to make sense of the information that the eye collected in the first thousandth of a second or so. If you stare, it is because you don't understand what you are looking at, not because you are seeing more. Perhaps now you can understand why the exact amount of time a person is allowed to view the letters in the rectangle doesn't matter very much, provided it is less than the fifth of a second or more required to organize a second glance.

If four or five random letters are the most that can be seen from a single glance, it might then appear that the question of how fast we can read would depend on the speed at which we can keep glancing at a page. But you can't speed up reading by accelerating the movements of the eyes. The limitation is not on the rate at which the eyes can pick up information, but on the rate at which the brain can deal with that information, to make sense of it. To examine the limited rate at which the brain can handle new visual information, we must probe a little deeper into the matter of how the visual system works.

FIXATIONS

Unless they are locked upon an object in motion that they are tracking, such as a bird in flight or a moving finger, the eyes don't move smoothly and continuously. Instead they jump sporadically from one point of focus to another. When you look around a room, for example, your eyes dart from place to place, picking up information from a different location every time they come to rest. The detective whose eyes sweep down a suspect from head to foot, picking up every incriminating detail, exists only in fiction. In real life the detective's gaze leaps from the suspect's nose, to the feet, to the hands, and back perhaps to the left leg before settling accusingly on the pocket in which the evidence is lodged. Incidentally, the fact that the eyes jump around when we examine a scene or object helps to make the point that you see with the brain, not the eyes. No matter how fast and in what order your eyes examine the different parts of a room, in your perception the room remains coherent and stable. You don't see the constantly changing and fragmented "image" that falls on the retina of the eye; you see the stationary room that the brain constructs. However incomplete and disjointed the information available at the eye, the brain organizes an integrated perceptual experience—if it can—that is complete and meaningful.

In reading, the eyes don't move smoothly along the lines and down the page. Once again the eyes shift around in leaps and bounds that in reading are given the technical label *saccades* (a French word meaning "jerks"). And in the jargon of reading, the periods when the eyes come to rest are called *fixations*, although the duration and function of fixations in reading are no different from those of the pauses that the eyes make in perceiving the world generally. Each fixation is a glance.

During the saccade, by the way, when the eyes are in motion, you are essentially blind, unaware of the blurred image that must sweep over the retina as the eyes move across a stationary scene. The blur is visual information that the brain ignores.

Shifting the eyes from one fixation point to another doesn't take very long. Depending on the angle through which the eyes have to travel, the time spent in movement ranges from a few thousandths of a second to about a tenth of a second. The average interval between fixations is about a quarter of a second, so that for most of the time the eyes are immobile. As I have already explained, only the beginning part of the fixation is taken up with the eye getting information from the page and into the visual system. For most of the duration of the fixation, the brain is busy interpreting. I have also said that the rate of reading can't be speeded up by accelerating changes of fixation. Both beginning and fluent readers change fixations about four times a second, which is about the rate at which children and adults glance quickly around a room or inspect a picture.

THE RATE OF VISUAL INFORMATION PROCESSING

To recapitulate, readers change their point of fixation about four times a second, and in a single fixation they can identify four or five letters out of a line of letters similar to those in the rectangle in our imaginary experiment. It might appear then that the rate at which the brain can process visual information is easily calculated: 5 letters per fixation multiplied by 4 fixations per second equals 20 letters per second. But such is not the case. The rate at which the brain can identify letters in the situation we have examined is only four or five letters per second. In other words, it takes the brain a full second to complete the identification of the four or five letters that can be seen in a single glance.

Researchers know that the brain requires a second to identify five letters from the visual information available from a single fixation because if they flash a second line of letters on the screen in their experiments within a second of the first, the two displays of visual information interfere with each other. If the second display of letters comes within about a tenth of a second of the first, an observer may even deny that the first display was ever presented. The longer the delay between the two displays, the more an observer is able to report seeing, but the full quota of four of five letters will not be reported from the first display unless the interval between the displays is a second or more. Obviously the visual information that the eyes can pick up in a thousandth of a second stays available to the brain for at least a second. But it doesn't look as if unprocessed visual information stays in the head any longer than a second, because there is no further improvement if the interval between the first and second displays is extended to 2 seconds, or 3 seconds, or indefinitely. Four or five random letters is the limit. To report more, the observer requires more information.

There is another kind of experimental technique that verifies the fact that individual letters can't be identified faster than four or five a second. Six-letter words are unreadable if the letters comprising them are flashed on a screen one at a time, always in the same position so that each successive letter "masks" the one before, at a rate faster than four or five a second. In other words, at least a fifth of a second is required for the identification of successive letters when the letters can only be seen one at a time.

So now we have answers to two questions raised in this chapter:

1. There is a limit to how much can be seen at any one time, and that limit in terms of random letters is four or five.
2. There is a limit to the rate at which the brain can identify random letters in reading, and that rate is four or five letters per second.

READING IS DIFFERENT

Regardless of the results that researchers claim to get in their experiments, you may object that real-life vision is different. Obviously we can read faster than four or five letters a second, which would work out to a maximum reading speed of barely 60 words a minute. And indeed we must be able to read faster, because 60 words a minute happens to be far too slow for reading with understanding. But I didn't say that the experiments demonstrated how fast we can read, only that the brain can deal with visual information no faster than the rate of four or five random letters a second. When we read we use nonvisual as well as visual information. Now I want to show that by using nonvisual information we can make the limited amount of visual information the brain can handle from a fixation go much further, and thus see and understand much more.

The imaginary experiment must be conducted again, still with a sequence of 25 letters presented to the eyes for no more than a single glance, therefore making available to the brain the same amount of visual information. But this time the 25 letters are not random; they are presented in the form of familiar but random words, as in the following example:

SNEEZE FURY HORSES WHEN AGAIN

Once again you must imagine having just one glance at the letters in the rectangle, either because they are flashed on a screen for just a fraction of a second or because they are revealed to you briefly by the movement of a covering card. Are you ready? There! What did you see? And the answer this time is: twice as much as you were able to see before. When the letters are organized into words, readers can generally identify a couple of words, the equivalent of 10 or 12 letters. You would probably have seen FURY HORSES or HORSES WHEN.

It isn't an adequate explanation of the previous phenomenon to say that in the second demonstration words were recognized instead of individual letters. Of course they were. But you never get something for nothing in reading, and in order to recognize the two words you had to employ visual information that must have been contained in the letters.

So we are left with the question of how the same amount of visual information that would permit you to identify only four or five unrelated letters enables you to identify twice as many letters if they are organized into random words. And the answer is that you must be making the same amount of *visual information* go twice as far. You are making use of *nonvisual information* that you already have in your brain and which in the present instance must be related to your knowledge of how written words are formed.

The essential point of the two demonstrations so far is that the amount of visual information required to identify a single letter is cut by half if the letter occurs in a word. The amount of visual information required to identify a letter of the alphabet is not fixed but depends on whether or not the letter is in a word. Identification of a letter involves the brain in a decision, and the amount of information required to make the decision depends on the number of alternatives there are. So now I have to show that the number of alternatives that a letter might be varies depending on its context. I also have to show that as readers we know how the number of alternatives can be reduced when letters occur in words and that indeed we can make use of this nonvisual information when we are called on to identify letters in words.

KNOWLEDGE ABOUT LETTERS

Suppose that instead of asking you to imagine trying to identify the original sequence of 25 random letters in a single glance, I had asked you to guess what each of those letters was likely to be, without looking at them at all. You could justifiably object that there was no way for you to guess that one letter would occur rather than any other. That is what the word *random* means—that each letter has an equal probability of occurring, namely 1 in 26. Any letter of that sequence could have been any letter of the alphabet. You had no basis for making an intelligent guess.

But now suppose that I had asked you to guess what a particular letter might be in that second sequence of letters, the letters that were arranged into random English words. Now you would have been in a position to make a more educated guess—you would probably have guessed E, or perhaps T or A or S. It is very unlikely that you would have guessed Y or X or Z. And your guess would have had a very sound basis, because, in fact, E, T, A, I, O, N, and S are by far the most frequent letters in English words, while Y, X, and Z are relative rarities. Individual letters are not all given the same amount of work to do in English words: E, for example, occurs 40 times more often than Z. Had you guessed E, you would have been 40 times more likely to be right than if you had guessed Z.

Now I'm not suggesting that we read words by blindly guessing what particular letters might be. But we can use our very accurate knowledge of what letters are likely to be in order to exclude from consideration those letters that are unlikely to occur. This is informed guessing, or prediction. By excluding unlikely letters in advance, we can reduce the number of alternatives the brain has to consider so that it processes very much less information. Of course we shall be wrong on occasion, but our knowledge of how letters go together to form English words is so extensive and so reliable that we can take the chance of being wrong occasionally in order to take advantage of the gains we make by guessing right so often.

Let me show how prediction can be based on sound prior knowledge. Play another guessing game with me. I'm thinking of a common six-letter word. What is the first letter likely to be? Most English speakers confronted by such a question guess one of the common letters I have already listed. In a number of informal demonstrations I have conducted with large groups of people, I have found that 1 in 4 or 1 in 5 guesses S—not 1 in 26, which is what the average would be if guesses were made randomly. Remember, what is important is not to guess exactly the letter I have in mind, but to guess a likely letter. And I get very few guesses of X or J or Z. Suppose, then, that the guess of S is correct—and indeed the six-letter word I have in mind does begin with S. What is the second letter likely to be?

Now it happens to be another fact of English spelling that letters don't follow each other at random in English words, even given their overall unequal frequencies in the language. E is the most common letter of the English language, but not after Q. Every experienced reader knows that if the first letter of a word is S, the next letter will almost certainly be a vowel or one of a limited set of consonants. The second letter of the word I have in mind happens to be T, which on average I find one person in three guesses correctly the first time. But I'm not so much concerned with the fact that one person in three is absolutely correct as that hardly anyone makes a ridiculous guess, like J or B. People use their knowledge of letters and words. They guess the most probable letters, which means that their chances of being correct are high. If the first two letters are S and T, what is the third? The third letter (which is R) has to be a vowel or Y or R, so we are down to seven alternatives, rather than 26. There are only six alternatives for the fourth letter, which happens to be E, and only two vowels and a few consonants for the fifth, which is A. STREA—can you guess what the last letter will be? Depending on the way you perceive the world (I'm conducting a cunning personality test), you will guess M or K.

Have I made the point? Statistical analyses of English words show that the average number of alternatives that a letter could be in English words is not 26, but 8. Occasionally there will be a large number of alternatives, of course, but sometimes hardly any. There is almost no question about the letter following a Q, for example, or the missing letters in the phrase "Pa_s t_e sug_r, pl_ _s_." In fact, every other letter can be obliterated from many passages of English text without affecting understanding at all. To be technical, English (like all languages) is highly redundant: there is usually much more information available to us than we need. Our uncertainty of what a letter might be depends on the number of alternatives, and every letter contains enough visual information to identify it from among 26 alternatives, or even more. But because of the redundancy in our language, our uncertainty about letters in English text is never as great as 1 in 26. What we already know about our language in advance reduces our uncertainty from 1 in 26 to an average of about 1 in 8.

Not only do all readers have this prior knowledge of their language—generally without being aware they have it—but also they constantly use the prior knowledge without being aware of it. This is why letters on distant billboards or letters that are scribbled may be impossible to identify in isolation but are quite clear in words. We have less uncertainty about what letters might be in words. Children who have been reading for less than a couple of years demonstrate the use of nonvisual information. They find it easier to identify letters that are obscured in some way when those letters are in words than when the identical letters are in sequences that don't constitute words.

Where does it come from, this very specialized skill that enables us to use prior knowledge about letter probabilities in reading, even though we may be unaware of both the knowledge and its use? The answer can only lie in reading itself. The acquisition and use of nonvisual information in reading are among the essential skills of reading that are never taught. They are developed without conscious effort, simply through reading. After all, children have been living since birth with the universal limitation on the amount of visual information that a brain can handle, and have solved the problem of identification with minimal information many times, in the process of recognizing familiar faces and objects in their world. If we are unaware of having this skill, it is because we perform it so well. Learning to acquire and use knowledge that will reduce the amount of visual information the brain must use is natural and inevitable.

NONVISUAL INFORMATION FROM SENSE

I have one more demonstration, this time to show that an additional aspect of nonvisual information can at least quadruple how much can be seen from a single input of visual information. Imagine once more the brief presentation of 25 letters, except that now they are arranged in a meaningful sequence of English words. Not only are the words grammatically organized, but they also make sense:

> EARLY FROSTS HARM THE CROPS

Are you ready? Once again, one glance is all you are allowed. How much did you see? And the usual result this time is everything. You didn't see just part of the line, but all of it, four or five words instead of four or five letters.

There should be no need to belabor the point. The amount of visual information available to the brain in each of my three demonstrations was the same, and each time the brain had the same amount of time to interpret the information. If at least four times as much can be seen when the letters form a sequence of words that makes sense, it must be that the sense makes so much nonvisual information available that the visual information can be made to go four times as far.

Now I must show that readers can indeed possess prior knowledge about how words go together in English that will cut down the number of alternatives dramatically, and therefore reduce the amount of information required to identify words.

Let us play a game of guessing successive words in sentences. Suppose I stop writing . . .

Can you guess what the next word was going to be in the interrupted sentence you have just read? If your guess was *in*, you were correct. What might the next word be after

Suppose I stop writing in . . .

Almost certainly you would have guessed the next word in that sequence:

Suppose I stop writing in the . . .

The next word was to have been *middle*. Then *of*, *a*, and *sentence*.

Such a demonstration takes up too much room in print. Try the experiment instead with a friend, reading a brief item in a newspaper or magazine and asking for predictions about each successive word.

I'm not concerned that you or your friend should get every word absolutely right in such a demonstration. Indeed, if you could predict every word exactly there would be no purpose in reading the passage in the first place. What is necessary is that every time you are always able to make a reasonable guess about the next word. You don't predict recklessly. You select from a relatively small set of possible words in the particular context, and as a result you cut down the number of alternatives among which the brain has to select. The gain is considerable.

An author can choose from at least 50,000, perhaps 100,000, words in writing a book, in the sense that most readers can recognize on sight and understand anywhere from 50,000 to 100,000 words. And each of these words from which the author can choose obviously contains sufficient visual information that it could be identified in isolation. Put another way, each word must contain sufficient visual information to be distinguished from 100,000 alternatives. But in making decisions about what a particular word in the book will be, the author can't choose from among 100,000 alternatives. The author can't say, "I haven't used the word *rhinoceros* for a long time, I'll use it now." Given what the author wants to say and the language in which it is being said, the number of available alternatives is always limited. The author also can't suddenly decide to use a past participle or the passive voice. The grammatical constructions that may be employed are also constrained by the sense of the message to be conveyed. In fact, at any particular point in the text, an author is free to choose not among about 100,000 words but among an average of about 250. It is knowledge of what the 250 alternatives might be for any particular word that enables readers to read and understand what the author has written.

Readers have nonvisual information about the choices available to the author, and they make full use of this knowledge to reduce their own uncertainty about what successive words might be. When I stopped in the middle of a sentence and invited guesses about what the next word might be, you (or your friend) would be very unlikely to have reasoned, "He hasn't used *rhinoceros* for a long time so I'll try that." The guess—the prediction—would have been for a word that was possible. In other words, you have a reasonable idea of what an author is going to write before you read it. You aren't identifying one word out of 100,000 every time, but one out of 200 or 300. And if you don't have that much expectation about what the next word might be, you won't be able to understand what you read, simply because you won't be reading fast enough or seeing enough at any one time. You may be reduced from seeing a meaningful four or five words in a fixation to seeing a meaningless four or five letters.

This reduction of uncertainty by the reader makes a tremendous difference to how much visual information has to be processed. As much visual information as you would need to identify a single letter in isolation will permit you to identify an entire word in a meaningful context. Perhaps you can't read the word *toast* if I scribble it by itself, but if I write "This morning I had *toast* and marmalade for breakfast," you will probably have little difficulty in deciphering it. You just don't need as much visual information when a word is in context.

In reasonably easy-to-read texts, such as newspaper or magazine articles, one letter in two or one complete word in five can be eliminated without affecting intelligibility. In other words, readers know so much that for every letter the author supplies, they can provide the next themselves, without even looking.

TUNNEL VISION

By way of review, let's look at the main points I've made so far in this chapter in the reverse order of the demonstrations.

There is a limit to the amount of visual information the brain can handle. How much can actually be seen and understood in a single glance, or in an entire second of visual information processing, depends on how much nonvisual information the brain can bring to bear. If a lot of nonvisual information is available to the brain, then an entire line of type can be apprehended at once:

If only a limited amount of nonvisual information can be used, however, only half as much can be seen:

And if there is practically no nonvisual information that can be used, then vision is restricted to a very small area indeed:

A graphic term is used to describe the condition illustrated in the third situation: *tunnel vision.* We see a line of print as if we were looking at it through a narrow paper tube.

Tunnel vision, you will notice, is not here a physical malfunction of the eyes, nor is it a consequence of any weakness in the visual system. Tunnel vision is not a permanent state; it occurs when the brain is overloaded with visual information. Tunnel vision is a condition in which beginning readers must often find themselves.

Tunnel vision isn't restricted to children, however. It isn't difficult to give adults tunnel vision, for example, by asking them to read something that they don't understand very well. Reading nonsense causes tunnel vision, for the simple reason that nonsense isn't predictable. Tunnel vision is, however, an occupational hazard of learning to read, partly because the beginner by definition doesn't have very much experience in reading. But the condition is aggravated if the print the beginner is expected to read isn't very predictable, so that little nonvisual information will be available in any case.

Tunnel vision is not restricted to reading; it will occur in any situation in which the brain has to process large amounts of visual information. The information-processing limitation applies to the ears as well as the eyes. It is easier to hear what someone is saying, even in a whisper or in a room where many conversations are going on at the same time, if what is being said makes sense to you. But nonsense is much harder to hear. It isn't for nothing that we raise our voices when we try to speak in an unfamiliar foreign language; difficulty in comprehension produces temporary hearing loss. Most teachers are familiar with children who appear to be deaf in class but can hear perfectly well outside.

CAUSES OF TUNNEL VISION

Because of the bottleneck in the visual-information-processing capacity of the brain, reading depends on using visual information economically, by utilizing as much nonvisual information as possible. But tunnel vision is unavoidable in the following circumstances:

1. *Trying to read something that makes no sense to you causes tunnel vision.* You should note that whether or not something is nonsense depends to a large extent on what the reader knows. If you could read Swedish, then you would have seen several words with each glance at the passage of Swedish that I gave you to read earlier in this chapter. But if the passage in Swedish was essentially random letters to you, then you would have had tunnel vision. The fact that a piece of writing makes sense to an adult, who can therefore see it easily, doesn't mean that the same passage will make sense to a child. If something can't be predicted, it will cause tunnel vision. Are the language and content of children's readers always predictable?

2. *Lack of relevant knowledge causes tunnel vision.* It isn't necessary to throw away a book because you find it unreadable. Acquisition of a little prior knowledge from elsewhere may suddenly make the book become readable. Students who have difficulty reading science or

history texts may not be suffering from a lack of reading ability. They may simply need to know a little more about science or history. Visual and nonvisual information are required for reading anything. If there is a lack of nonvisual information, then the reader must seek elsewhere to acquire it.

3. *Reluctance to use nonvisual information causes tunnel vision.* Using nonvisual information involves risk—there is always a chance you might be wrong. But if you aren't making occasional errors when you read, you're probably not reading efficiently. You are relying on more visual information than you need. Errors needn't be a cause for concern in reading, provided the reader is using appropriate nonvisual information. Such a reader reads for meaning. And if we read for meaning and make a mistake, then the sense of the passage usually alerts us if the mistake we have made makes a difference. (If a mistake makes no difference, then what difference can it make?) Thus a good reader is likely to make quite conspicuous misreadings sometimes, like reading *apartment* rather than *house*. And such a reader won't self-correct unless the misreading makes a difference to meaning. This is the way fluent readers read. A poor reader, on the other hand, might pay far more attention to visual aspects of the task and mistakenly read *horse* for *house*. Such a reader won't be likely to self-correct, although this time the error makes a considerable difference to sense, because the meaning isn't being attended to in the first place. A common characteristic of poor readers in high school is that they read as if they don't expect what they read to make sense, as if getting every individual word right was the key to reading. But the more they try to get every word right, the less they will see, the less they will understand, and the worse their reading will be on every count.

   The greatest cause of reluctance to use nonvisual information sufficiently is anxiety. In any situation in life, the more anxious we are about the consequences of a decision, the more information we require before that decision is made. And in reading, you just can't stop to collect large amounts of visual information in order to make your decisions. Anxiety causes tunnel vision, and tunnel vision eliminates any likelihood of comprehension.

4. *Poor reading habits cause tunnel vision.* If you read too slowly you will get tunnel vision, since the visual system will become clogged with all the visual information you are trying to get from the page. If

you are reluctant to push ahead, reading and rereading in a hapless endeavor to remember every detail, then you will get tunnel vision. If you strive to get every word right before you look at the next, you will get tunnel vision. Unfortunately, these bad reading habits are sometimes deliberately taught in the belief that they will help children read. The problem for many children who experience difficulty in becoming readers is not that they can't learn, but that they learn too readily. They have been influenced too much by an adult who misguidedly says, "Slow down, be careful, and make sure you get every word right."

OVERCOMING TUNNEL VISION

Cures become obvious once causes are apparent. Might children have tunnel vision because what they are expected to read is nonsense to them? Then the teacher should ensure that what the children are expected to read makes sense to them. A "readability formula" or "grade-level" classificatory scheme won't be a reliable guide for teachers; the problem is too relative. What is lucid to one child may be completely unpredictable to another. But there is a simple solution. If children can't understand something even if it is read to them, there is no way they will make sense of it when trying to read it for themselves.

Might children have tunnel vision because they have insufficient prior knowledge of what they are required to read? Then they must be given the necessary prior knowledge in some other way: from other books that they can read, from a discussion or a film, or even from having some or all of the book they are expected to read read for them first. Reading ability won't be improved by tasks that are discouraging or impossible.

Might children have tunnel vision because they are afraid of making mistakes? Neither comprehension nor learning can take place successfully in an atmosphere of anxiety. Prediction, like learning, can be a risky business, and a child must feel that the risks are worth taking. Children who are afraid to make a mistake won't learn and won't even demonstrate the reading ability that they might have acquired. Reassurance must be the basis of "remedial" instruction for readers experiencing difficulties at any age.

Might a reader have tunnel vision because of poor reading habits? The secret of all speed-reading courses is fundamentally to force the reader to read quickly. Many readers go slowly because they are afraid they won't comprehend if they speed up. Speed-reading courses aim to show that fast reading is efficient reading. Their students are forced into situations in which tunnel vision is impossible; the reassurance they get as their vision and comprehension open up provides the basis for more efficient reading generally.

SUMMARY

We don't see everything that is in front of our eyes, and we see nothing immediately. It takes time for the brain to decide what the eyes are looking at. Reading depends more on what is behind the eyes—on nonvisual information—than on the visual information in front of them. Excessive reliance on visual information can overwhelm the brain's decision-making ability and result in tunnel vision, when only a few letters rather than entire phrases can be seen at one time. Tunnel vision is most likely to occur when what is read makes little sense to the reader or when the reader is anxious about making mistakes. Neither closer attention to the text nor increasing the fixation rate will make reading more efficient or make learning to read easier.

CHAPTER 5

Bottlenecks of Memory

There's another reason why reading must depend on the eyes as little as possible: If we are too concerned with the print in front of us, we will probably forget what we are reading as we read it. I'm not talking about being unable to recall what we have read an hour or a day or a week later, though this is an aspect of memory I will discuss later in this chapter. I'm talking about forgetting what we read immediately, so that we can't even understand it, let alone recall it subsequently. I'm talking about forgetting the beginning of a sentence before we get to the end of it, so that it can make no sense. Or even—if we are unfortunate enough to be afflicted with tunnel vision—forgetting the beginning of a word before we get to the end, so that we can't even decide what a particular word is.

Forgetting where you are in the middle of a word is not an uncommon phenomenon. We all experience it occasionally when we try to read or pronounce long words in a language or technical vocabulary that is unfamiliar to us. The same difficulty arises when we can't get past the middle of a complex mathematical formula, or fail to remember completely a new address or telephone number when we have nowhere immediately convenient to write it down. In each of these cases, the kind of memory that seems to be overwhelmed isn't the memory that we call on when we want to recollect something that happened days or months ago. Rather it's a more temporary memory that is required so that we can make sense of what we are doing at the moment. This kind of "instant memory" is called *short-term memory*, to distinguish it from our *long-term memory* of events long past. Both kinds of memory are important in reading. Both have limitations as well as strengths. I shall talk first about short-term memory and then about long-term memory.

LIMITATIONS OF SHORT-TERM MEMORY

Short-term memory can be very easily overloaded, or overwhelmed, and a sure way to do this in reading is to try to fill short-term memory with too much detailed information from the text.

Information about the world around us flows into and out of short-term memory all the time we are conscious, even though we aren't normally aware of the process at all. But if someone you were listening to suddenly stopped and asked, "What were the last half-dozen words I said?" you could always give the answer, provided you had been paying attention. Suddenly cover the page or close the book while you are reading, and you will find that you can always recapitulate the last few words you have read. Ask someone who is watching a sporting event or a film for a description of the most recent action, and it can usually be provided. Always there seems to be a residue of the immediate past in the forefront of our mind that we can recover if we are asked, although we are rarely aware of having it. This "instant playback" of the immediate past is short-term memory; it's not very different from what is often called attention. Short-term memory is, in fact, everything we happen to be paying attention to right now, including our own intentions.

Incidentally, these examples all show that in one sense memorization is never a problem at all. Everything to which we are paying attention seems to get into the head briefly. The difficulty isn't memorization but forgetting—the information that gets into the mind doesn't stay or we can't find it when we want it.

Forgetting isn't usually a problem with short-term memory, however, because we rarely want the information it contains to stay for very long—only while we make sense of what we are doing or complete what we are trying to accomplish. We may want to remember the words at the beginning of a sentence until we get to the end of it, but no longer. Imagine the clutter in your head if you remembered every word you saw or heard, no matter how trivial or irrelevant it might be. Short-term memory clears itself automatically to allow us to proceed with the next item of business.

Short-term memory, in other words, is our *working memory*, which briefly holds what we happen to be attending to. It then clears so that we can continue with the next task. It's rather like an internal scratchpad where we jot down a few notes relevant to a current problem and then erase so that we can work on the next one.

Human short-term memory is such an efficient system that we are rarely aware of its limitations and therefore rarely aware that it exists. Short-term memory does have shortcomings, however. There is a limit to how much it can hold and a limit to how long its contents can be retained.

Suppose you have just looked up a new number in the telephone directory and try to dial the number without a second look in the book. You usually find that you can just about hold the seven-digit sequence in your mind, provided you don't have to give any attention to anything else. If someone asks if you have the correct time, the telephone number disappears. If the operator asks for your own number, you lose track of the one you are trying to call. Short-term memory, in other words, has a capacity for about six or seven items—enough for a telephone number but not an unfamiliar area code as well; enough for a five-digit but not a nine-digit zip code.

Short-term memory also has a very limited duration. We can remember the six or seven items only as long as we give all our attention to them. The technical term for the deliberate way in which we try to keep something in short-term memory is *rehearsal*. We can retain the unfamiliar telephone number for just as long as we are able to rehearse it. The moment we turn even part of our attention elsewhere, something is lost.

Conversely, for as long as we pay attention to what is in short-term memory, we can't attend to anything else. Once again we will be essentially blind, even with our eyes open, if we pay so much attention to detail that we have no room left in short-term memory. The contents of short-term memory represent our complete experiential world at any particular time. If we want to make sense of what we are attending to at that particular time, we must be able to make sense of the contents of short-term memory.

Perhaps you can now see why tunnel vision in reading is such a disaster for short-term memory. Earlier, you might have thought that the problem of tunnel vision could be easily overcome; if you can see only four or five letters at a glance rather than four or five words, then all you need do is read slower. But anyone who can identify only four or five letters in a fixation will find that they just about fully occupy short-term memory, given that short-term memory is probably also occupied with the general control of the reading task. There is no way that any reader will be able to comprehend if attention is restricted to four or five letters at a time, perhaps forgetting E-L-E-P while working on H-A-N-T, or losing track of the first half of a sentence before getting into the second half. Comprehension gets lost in the bottleneck of short-term memory the moment we worry about getting individual words right or become afraid that we might miss a significant detail.

OVERCOMING LIMITATIONS OF SHORT-TERM MEMORY

It may sound as if I'm arguing that reading is impossible, if roughly half a dozen items is the most we can hold in short-term memory at any one time, and attention to four or five or even six letters isn't enough to enable us to make sense of print. How is the bottleneck overcome? The answer must be that reading isn't a matter of identifying individual letters, or even individual words. When we are reading with comprehension, we must not be bothering short-term memory with letters or even words at all. We avoid overloading short-term memory by paying minimal attention to all the incidental detail of print.

Recall my earlier observations about the limited capacity of short-term memory. I said it could hold no more than six or seven items, but I didn't say what those items had to be. Short-term memory will just about hold the seven digits of an unfamiliar telephone number, or it will hold the same number of unrelated letters. But it will also hold half a dozen *words*. And if we can put half a dozen words into short-term memory, then we can in effect retain 25 or 30 letters. We can make short-term memory look much more efficient if we can organize small items into larger units. This organization is sometimes referred to as *chunking*. The capacity of short-term memory isn't so much six or seven items as six or seven chunks. A word is a chunk of letters. I can give you a chunk of a dozen digits that you could easily hold in short-term memory and still have capacity left over for more: 123456123456 or 888888888888. Will the letters CHEVAL fill short-term memory for you? It depends on whether you understand French. If you know that CHEVAL means "horse," you will have room in short-term memory for CHEVAL and five or six other items. But if CHEVAL is meaningless to you, then short-term memory will be filled.

Now you have another reason why comprehension is so important in reading and in learning to read. A *chunk* is a meaningful organization of elements; it is, in fact, something you know already. The reason the word HORSE is so much easier to hold in short-term memory than the same number of unrelated letters, or that 1234567 is easier than 7425163, is that you are familiar with the sequences already. It's not so much that the letters or digits are ordered that makes them easier to attend to as the fact that you are familiar with the order; you have it in your head already, so you don't have to put it all in short-term memory. The familiar organization is another aspect of nonvisual information. You overcome the limitations of short-term memory in reading by making the most sense you can out of what you are looking at. You don't worry about letters if you can make sense of words. Worrying about letters will make word identification difficult; trying to read nonsense will make reading impossible.

SHORT-TERM MEMORY AND MEANING

I have said that the capacity of short-term memory is six or seven *chunks,* which may be six or seven letters or six or seven words. But we can hold units larger than words in short-term memory; we can fill it with rich chunks of meaning. Now it's difficult to say exactly how big a "meaning" is because meanings are not amenable to being separated and counted or measured in the way letters and words are. And it takes a little time to explain what meanings are because it's in the nature of meanings that they go far beyond mere words, a complication that will be the topic of following chapters. But it's not difficult to demonstrate that we can hold meanings in short-term memory instead of individual words, and that the equivalent of many more than six or seven words can be held in short-term memory if they are organized meaningfully.

For example, the limitation to six or seven on the number of words that can be held at one time in short-term memory only applies when the words are truly independent, unrelated items: a "list" of words such as *imagine, with, who, begun, the, forget, contents.* But if the words form a meaningful sentence, at least a dozen can often be recalled without error. And sentences of 20 words or more can usually be repeated immediately after a single hearing, not perfectly but at least with no omissions or changes that affect the basic meaning—compelling evidence that it's meaning rather than the particular words that we hold in short-term memory.

The only efficient way to read is at the level of meaning, and the only way to learn to read is at the same level. Unfortunately, students are often expected to read material that isn't meaningful to them (no matter how much sense it makes to the teacher). Moreover, children are often expected to learn to read with material that isn't meaningful to anyone. Some producers of instructional materials even make a virtue out of the fact that their products are nonsense, saying that it inhibits children from committing the supposed offense of "guessing." But all that nonsense does and can do is cause tunnel vision and a logjam in short-term memory. (I'm not, of course, referring to nonsense in the sense of absurdity or ridiculousness, which everyone can enjoy when it can be related to circumstances we understand. I'm referring to events that have no possibility of making sense to us, no matter how much we stretch our imagination.)

Material that is meaningful—that can be related to what a child or student already knows—is essential if reading skill is to be developed. But meaningfulness may not be enough. One of the tragedies of some reading instruction is that children are sometimes encouraged to read sense as if it were nonsense. They are told to make sure to get all the individual words right, and to slow down and figure out the hard words letter by letter when they run into difficulty. The problem with this type of instruction is that all too often it is effective: Children learn that reading isn't a matter of making sense but of getting every word right. Older students characterized as having severe reading problems typically behave as if they have no expectation that what they are trying to read will make sense. They have learned too well the destructive lesson that comprehension should take second place to word accuracy. Being able to recognize words on sight is a skill that comes *with* reading; it's not a prerequisite *for* reading. Like any kind of sight recognition—birds, stars, cars, airplanes, trees—it comes with experience.

LIMITATIONS OF LONG-TERM MEMORY

Short-term memory alone would scarcely be sufficient for all our needs. It may be uniquely adapted for holding a telephone number that we intend to call in the next minute or so, but we can hardly rehearse a number continuously if we don't plan to dial it for a week. Short-term memory is the location for information that we intend to erase. But what about information that we want to keep? The knowledge and beliefs that are part of our more or less permanent understanding of the world are contained within a different aspect of memory that is called long-term. Long-term memory is the source of the all-important nonvisual information in reading that I have been talking about.

Long-term memory is different in several respects from short-term memory. At first glance it even seems to compensate for all the shortcomings of short-term memory. For example, short-term memory has very limited capacity—six or seven items or chunks—but the capacity of long-term memory appears to be literally inexhaustible. No one need ever fear to learn something in case long-term memory is fully occupied already. There is no need to erase from your mind the name of an old friend to make room for the name of a new one. Long-term memory seems always able to expand to accommodate new information that we want to put into it.

Moreover, the contents of long-term memory seem to persist indefinitely. While the contents of short-term memory slip away the moment our attention is distracted, nothing in long-term memory seems ever to be forgotten. Sometimes events that we haven't thought about for years are suddenly brought to mind, perhaps by an old photograph or a snatch of song, or by a particular taste or smell. All our senses seem capable of revivifying memories we might have thought we had lost forever.

You might object that long-term memory may be boundless and permanent in theory, but in practice it's often difficult to recall things that you tried to memorize even quite recently. But there is a distinction between *memorization*, or getting something into long-term memory, and *retrieval*, getting it out again. Here we confront the first great limitation of long-term memory, the fact that its contents are rarely immediately accessible.

Unlike information in short-term memory, which is instantly available for recall, information in long-term memory requires positive action to get it out. It can be most frustrating when we have almost recovered something we want from long-term memory but still it manages to elude us. What was the name of that restaurant that served such delicious desserts? You know it was a two-syllable word, and it probably began with a K, but the rest is tantalizingly out of reach. Was it the Kingsway? No—but how can you tell what a memory is not, if you can't tell what it is? Obviously the memory is there, locked away in some manner, but you haven't found a key that fits. One of the keys would be the sought-for word itself. The moment somebody gives you the correct name, or you suggest it to yourself by running through possibilities, you are able to say, "Aha, that's it."

The critical difference between short-term and long-term memory can be summed up in one word: *organization*. Short-term memory holds unrelated items, but long-term memory is a network, a structure of knowledge; it is coherent. Long-term memory is everything we know about the world, and everything we know about the world is organized. We not only know that there are 26 letters in the alphabet, we also know their names, their order, and how they go together to form words. Our friend George is a teacher, like several other people we can name, and he has a dog that we know must have four legs and a tail. We can assume that George, being a teacher, knows there are 26 letters in the alphabet, but that his dog does not. Everything we know is related to everything else. Try to think of two things that can't be related in terms of a third. Nothing in our knowledge of the world can be completely unrelated to anything else that we know; it could not be "knowledge" if it were.

When we add to our knowledge of the world—when we learn—we either modify or elaborate the organization of information that we already have in long-term memory. Organization, in other words, is synonymous with "making sense." Anything we try to learn that can't be related to the structure of knowledge we already have in long-term memory is meaningless to us. It is nonsense. And there are several good reasons why no one should ever be in the position of having to try to learn or memorize something that is nonsense. One reason is this: It is only through organization that information can become established in long-term memory, and it is only through organization that it can be retrieved again.

Organization is the key to recall, as every student who has struggled to memorize a list of "facts" ought to know. To recall anything, you have to get to it through the network. You must probe among the kinds of things it might be related to. To get the name of the restaurant, try in your imagination to walk along the street it was located on. See if you can "see" the sign or the menu. The better we have something organized in long-term memory, the easier it is to retrieve. That is why recent events, especially those that happen to be particularly relevant to us, are usually easier to recall; they are more closely related to so many of our immediate concerns. The reason most of the memories of our childhood seem to have gone, except for the rare occasion when some particular stimulus quite unpredictably jogs our recollection, is that we view the world now with a different frame of reference. We have lost contact with our younger days. To recall what the world was like as a child, it must be seen through the eyes of a child.

This matter of the organization of knowledge in long-term memory will occupy us again, at greater length, when we consider the nature of meaning and comprehension. But for the moment we shouldn't be diverted any longer from our examination of the differences between short-term and long-term memory, for we have come to the most critical one of all: The rate at which new information can be put into long-term memory is very slow indeed.

Short-term memory, you will recall, has a limited and transient capacity, but at least information goes in and can be brought out practically instantaneously. You should start rehearsing the moment you find out the telephone number that you want to ring because the number is in short-term memory as soon as you have read it or heard it. But entry into long-term memory is laborious and time-consuming—it takes 4 or 5 seconds for one item to become established in long-term memory. To put a telephone number into long-term memory, so that you can recall it after lunch or in a week's time, requires a good half-minute of concentration, 4 or 5 seconds for every digit.

Now you can see why long-term memory can't be employed to make up for the limited capacity of short-term memory. To transfer even a single letter or word into long-term memory requires 5 seconds of concentration, an ultimate bottleneck that seals the fate of any attempt to read that involves an overemphasis on visual information.

This final bottleneck explains why the effort to memorize can completely destroy comprehension in reading. Every time you try to cram another detail into long-term memory, so that you may be able to answer some of those awkward questions afterward, you distract your attention from the text for at least 5 seconds. In such circumstances comprehension is impossible, and if you are trying to read without comprehension, what use is memorization in any case?

OVERCOMING LIMITATIONS OF LONG-TERM MEMORY

I have been as imprecise in talking about long-term memory as I was with short-term; I have been saying that you can put only one "item" into long-term memory every 5 seconds. But just as an item for short-term memory may be a letter, a word, or even a meaning, so an item for long-term memory can be a chunk as large as we can meaningfully make it.

Obviously reading will be disrupted if we try constantly to feed into long-term memory isolated and unrelated bits of information like single letters or individual words. But meanings (the meaning of a sentence or the meaning of a paragraph) can go into long-term memory as well, and it takes no longer to put a rich and relevant chunk of meaning into long-term memory than it does a useless letter or word.

The way to overcome the bottleneck of long-term memory, therefore, is the same as the solution to the problem of limited capacity in short-term memory and to the problem of tunnel vision in processing visual information: The material that you are reading must make sense to you in as meaningful a way as possible.

I must now briefly introduce two points that are relevant at this time but will be discussed in more detail later. The first is that it shouldn't be necessary to put a lot of new information into long-term memory when we read. There is a difference between comprehending something and committing it to memory. We make use of information that we already have in long-term memory in order to comprehend, but because of the bottleneck we don't bother to put into long-term memory a second time anything we already know. That is one reason we usually have a relatively poor recollection of books that are easily comprehensible, the relaxing paperbacks that don't make us think very much. They are easily comprehensible because they are largely predictable. We know a good deal about them in advance, and therefore we don't commit very much to memory. I'm not saying we shouldn't remember major points of what we read, although I believe memorization is rarely as important as many teachers insist. But it must be recognized that memorization exacts its price in reading. To expect a good deal of memorization, especially of material that isn't easily comprehensible in the first place, is to place a very high demand on a reader indeed.

My second point, I'm happy to say, is considerably more positive. Having stressed how the effort to memorize will interfere with comprehension, I can now present the other side of the coin: Comprehension takes care of memorization. The best justification for the preceding statement is to describe an actual memory experiment.

Three groups of people are put into exactly the same experimental situation. Each individual is given a pack of 50 index cards to study for a fixed period of time, say 20 minutes. On each card is a common word, a "concept" like *horse, tree, butterfly, justice,* or *running.* People in the first group are told simply to sort the cards into separate piles on any organizational basis they like. There are no restrictions, provided they make at least two piles and fewer than 50. In other words, members of this group are expected to think about the words on the cards. Asking them to sort the words in some manner is a cunning way of asking them to relate words on the basis of what they already know, to make the words meaningful. The actual manner in which the cards are organized is in fact irrelevant to the study and isn't examined, because the researchers are really concerned with memory. An hour after the conclusion of the 20-minute sorting task, when the participants think the experiment is over, the real purpose is suddenly thrust upon them. They are asked to recall as many of the 50 words as they can.

Unfair, you may say. If the purpose of the study is memorization, why not tell the participants what to expect? This is precisely what is done with the second group. They are given exactly the same cards and the same sorting task, but they are also warned in advance that a memorization test will follow. But this additional instruction makes no difference. The group that is required to memorize as well as to organize does no better on the memory task than the group that is simply asked to organize. In other words, the organization—the comprehension—takes care of the memorization.

Perhaps you will now object that the second group is asked to do too much, to organize as well as memorize. A third group in these experiments is not given the "irrelevant" task at all, but is simply told to examine the cards for 20 minutes because an hour later they will be given the memory task. They have the worst recollection of all. Simply trying to memorize results in the least memorization.

MEMORIZATION AND ANXIETY

So far I have emphasized meaningfulness. I have asserted that memory bottlenecks can be overcome in the same way as the visual bottleneck, by reading material that makes sense. But there are also questions of attitude.

A piece of reading material may be capable of making eminent sense to prospective readers yet still prove impossible for them to read. One reason, as in the case of tunnel vision, may be anxiety. Readers who are afraid of making a mistake as they read, of not comprehending every detail, will overload short-term memory and confuse themselves into complete bewilderment. And readers who try to cram too much into long-term memory will not only find that they have little to remember for their efforts, but also succeed in transmuting sense into nonsense in the process.

Why should any reader be so anxious about memorization that any possibility of comprehension, let alone enjoyment, is destroyed? One has only to consider the emphasis on tests and memorization in many school situations to find an answer. Indeed, the common procedure known in schools as a "comprehension test" is usually an imposition on long-term memory, since it is given when the reading is over. The emphasis on memorization damages the very thing the test is supposed to measure. High school students desperately anxious about their own reading ability may be given a free choice of books by well-meaning instructors and sent off with the blessing, "Just relax and enjoy it—I'll only ask you one or two general questions when you've finished." Now imagine the students trying to second-guess the instructor, trying to retain a mass of unimportant detail in the vain hope of covering the "one or two general questions" that might be asked. The innocuous request "Just tell me what the book is about," may prove no less monstrous, like "Summarize *War and Peace* in a couple of well-chosen sentences."

Unreasonable demands by others when we learn to read may lead to inappropriate reading habits later. Many adults seem to read—even when they are alone and "reading for pleasure"—as if they expect a sadistic examiner to trap them on every trivial point when they are finished. If they have trouble comprehending a sentence, they go back and reread it 10 times rather than go forward to ignore or even resolve the uncertainty.

No one who is afraid of the consequences of reading will be able to read, and no one who is afraid of failing to read will learn to read. A sure way to give learners a reading problem is to tell them that they have one.

But there is more to reading than vision and memory, necessary and important though they both are. There is more to reading even than a tranquil state of mind. We have still only looked at reading from inside the head, through the reader's eyes, so to speak. It's time to change the perspective and look at a completely different aspect of reading: its function as language.

SUMMARY

Short-term memory is a transient store for what we happen to be attending to at any particular time. *Long-term memory* is our relatively permanent knowledge of the world. Both aspects of memory have critical limitations that can disrupt reading and learning to read. Only a few things can be held in short-term memory at any one time, handicapping any reader who relies on visual information. Entry of new information into long-term memory is slow, and it interferes with comprehension. Both limitations are easily overcome if the reading material is meaningful, provided also that the reader isn't unduly anxious about making mistakes or about failing to remember details. For learners especially, it is crucial that reading materials make sense.

CHAPTER 6

Language and Meaning

The shortcomings of phonics and the bottlenecks of the visual system and memory are not the only reasons readers must not rely too exclusively on the print in front of their eyes. There is a third reason: It is not in print that the meaning of written language lies. Readers must bring meaning to print rather than expect to receive meaning *from* it. There is a difference between the visual information of print that we see on a page and meaning.

It is not in print—nor even in speech—that the meaning of language lies. If there is to be any understanding, it must come from the meaning that a listener or reader brings to the language being attended to. To explain the paradox and also its resolution, it is necessary to plunge a little deeper into the nature of language itself.

TWO ASPECTS OF LANGUAGE

There are two ways in which we can talk about language, whether spoken or written, and these two ways have nothing at all to do with each other. On the one hand, we can talk about the physical characteristics of language—about the loudness or duration of a passage of speech, or about the size of type or number of letters in a piece of written text. On the other hand, we can talk about meaning.

When we want to talk about the physical characteristics of language, references to meaning aren't merely unnecessary, they are irrelevant. If you assert that someone has just been talking loudly for five minutes, I can't object that the loudness and length of the speech would depend on whether the topic was bananas or battleships. A sentence printed in italic type is printed in italic type, whether or not it is perceived as true or false. To make statements about the physical characteristics of language, it's not necessary to specify or even know the particular language concerned. Statements about meaning, on the other hand, can be made quite independently of any statements about physical characteristics. A critical remark is a critical remark, whether it is spoken or written. A lie doesn't become truth by being shouted rather than whispered, or by being printed in one font rather than another.

It is a little awkward to have to use the phrase "the physical characteristics of spoken and written language" whenever the topic is language in general, but there is a useful expression we can employ in its place; we can talk of *surface structure*. The surface structure of speech might be regarded as the sound waves that pass through the air, or along telephone lines, from your vocal apparatus to my ears; it can be easily quantified by clocks and other measuring devices. The surface structure of written language can also be measured in a variety of ways; it is the ink marks on the page, the chalk marks on the board, or the pixels on the computer screen. The surface structure of written language is the visual information that our eyes pick up in their fixations in reading.

Surface structure is contrasted with *deep structure*, which is an alternative term for meaning. The metaphorical difference between deep and surface structure is particularly appropriate, since meaning—deep structure—lies at a level far below the superficial aspects of language. There is far more to language and its comprehension than is immediately apparent to the eye or ear at the shallower levels of print or sound. In fact, there is a good deal in the deep structure of language that is not in the surface structure at all. Surface structure and deep structure are not mirror images of each other. There is no one-to-one correspondence between the two. They aren't opposite sides of the same coin. A gulf separates them. The physical aspects of language, the print or the sound, contain insufficient information to convey meaning completely and unambiguously.

THE GULF BETWEEN SURFACE STRUCTURE AND MEANING

It is easy to demonstrate the absence of a direct correspondence between surface structure and deep structure: One surface structure may have more than one deep structure, and one deep structure may have more than one surface structure. Put another way, differences in meaning can exist with no difference in the physical characteristics of language, and the physical characteristics of language may vary without any difference in meaning.

An example of a surface structure with more than one deep structure is: *Visiting teachers may be boring.* Who is visiting, the teachers or the person being bored? The same printed words have two meanings. Intonation will do nothing to disambiguate the previous sentence, or any of the following: *The chicken was too hot to eat; sailing boats can be a pleasure; she runs through the sand and waves; the shooting of the hunters was terrible; father is roasting in the kitchen; mother was seated by the bishop; Cleopatra was rarely prone to argue.*

In the preceding examples, every sentence could be interpreted in more than one way; no surface structure corresponded uniquely to a single deep structure. The argument doesn't depend on the fact that I might have seemed to have specially picked a few unusual and not particularly entertaining puns. Ambiguity is a constant and unavoidable facet of all our language (and it will be revealing to consider, as we do later in the chapter, why readers or listeners are so rarely aware that this ambiguity exists).

To show that a single deep structure, a single meaning, can be represented by more than one surface structure requires no strain at all. Any paraphrases will make the point: *The dog chased the cat* and *the cat was chased by the dog* are quite different surface structures, but they represent the same meaning. So does *le chien a chassé le chat* and innumerable other sentences that could be composed in English and in other languages. The fact that any statement can be translated, and even paraphrased in the same language, illustrates the point made in the chapter on memory: Meaning lies beyond mere words. It makes sense to say that *he is unmarried* and *he is a bachelor* have the same meaning, but not to ask for another sentence that somehow crystallizes the meaning of both statements.

UNDERSTANDING SENTENCES

How, then, are sentences to be understood? If meaning is not inherent in surface structure, and surface structure is all that passes between writers and readers (or between speakers and listeners), where does meaning come from? The only possible answer is that readers or listeners must provide meaning themselves. To justify such an answer, it will help to examine in a little more detail why conventional explanations of language comprehension can't work.

The most common explanation of how sentences are understood is probably that we put together the meanings of the individual words. But comprehension can't be as simple as that, otherwise there would be no difference between a *Maltese cross* and a *cross Maltese,* or between a *Venetian blind* and a *blind Venetian.* The saying *Time flies* could be taken as a reference to a type of pest that infests clocks and watches, as fruit flies do fruit, or as an instruction to an official at an insect race meeting. *Hot dogs* could be overheated canines. Evidently we are doing more when we understand a sentence than putting together the meanings of each word. And the difference can't simply be a matter of the order in which the words occur. The first word of *Man the boats* and the first word of *Man is gregarious* are the same, but they have quite different meanings. Rather than the words giving meaning to sentences, it looks as if the sentences are giving meaning to the words.

It can't be argued that order plus grammar accounts for the meaning, because grammar itself often can't be determined until some meaning is allocated to the sentence. To know the different grammatical functions of the first words in *Man the boats* and *Man is gregarious,* the entire sentences must be understood. *Flies* is a verb in *time flies* and a noun in *fruit flies.* Is *Mother was seated by the bishop* a passive sentence (meaning the bishop showed mother to her seat) or is it an active sentence (meaning she was sitting beside him)? Only when you know what the sentence is supposed to mean can you say what the grammar is.

The underlying problem in all the previous examples is that words themselves have too many meanings. Just think of some of the common words of our language: *table* (dining or multiplication?), *chair* (a seat or an office?), *office* (place or position?), *club* (weapon or organization?), *sock* (clothing or blow?). These words were not specially selected for their multiple meanings. The difficulty is to think of words that do not have more than one sense. Once a word gets into common use, it tends to be given as many meanings as possible; this is a characteristic of all the world's languages and seems to reflect the way the human brain works best, using a few elements very productively rather than using many elements in a restricted manner. To confirm the point, just check in the dictionary for common words like *come, go, take, run, walk, house,* and *hand,* and see how many different meanings they have, often running to several columns, compared with the two- or three-line definitions required by less familiar words. You can't even tell the grammatical functions of many common words when you take them in isolation—*sock, run, walk, house, fence, bottle*. All can be verbs as well as nouns. Many other words can be nouns and adjectives (*automatic, green, cold*), or verbs and adjectives (*narrow, double, idle, empty*). Some words can have three grammatical functions (*paper, light, sound*).

The most common words in English are prepositions, and these are used with the greatest number of senses. One dictionary lists 63 different senses each for the words *of, at,* and *by*. These words are just about untranslatable from one language to another, unless you understand at least the phrase in which they occur. The meaning of the word *by* is obvious each of the five times it occurs in the sentence *I found the book by Dickens by chance by the tree and shall return it by mail by Friday*—but could you say what the word *by* means?

BRIDGING THE GULF

To summarize, neither individual words, their order, nor even grammar itself, can be appealed to as the source of meaning in language and thus of comprehension in reading. Nor is it possible to decode from the meaningless surface structure of writing into the sounds of speech in order to find a back route into meaning. The ambiguities I have discussed occur in speech just as much as in writing. Instead, some comprehension of the whole is required before one can say how individual words should sound, or deduce their meaning in particular utterances, or even assert their grammatical function. I'm not saying that an utterance can be taken to mean anything; with most utterances only one interpretation is intended and usually there is little argument about the interpretation that should be made. But this agreement doesn't explain how decisions about meaning are reached and how the essential ambiguity of surface structure is overcome.

Clearly, ambiguity poses no problem at all for producers of language. Presumably speakers and writers have a reasonable idea of what they want to say, and provided they produce a surface structure that is not incompatible with their intentions, they never suspect that their words might have some alternative interpretation. This is why speakers and writers are so often surprised when their audience doesn't find their remarks transparently clear. Speakers and writers are the last people to be aware of the puns they may unintentionally produce, or of the distortions of their meanings that are possible, and they tend to be embarrassed and even annoyed when these "misinterpretations" of what they say are pointed out to them. Meaning is self-evident when we are speaking and writing, and it is difficult to accept that it doesn't reside limpidly in our words but rather is lodged securely and perhaps even impenetrably in our heads.

How, then, does the recipient of language manage to attribute meaning to speech or written text? Why is it that readers and listeners are usually no more aware of possible ambiguity than the writer or speaker who produces the language they comprehend? There can be only one answer: In reading or listening we approach language from the same perspective that we employ when we write or speak—the meaning must come first. If the discussion is about logarithms or transportation schedules, we never consider that *table* might refer to a piece of furniture. If the topic is horticultural blight, we don't even contemplate that *fruit flies* might be a noun and a verb. *Harold is cooking in the kitchen* must mean that Harold is doing the cooking; *Cabbage is cooking in the kitchen* must mean that cabbage is being cooked. Listeners often have as much trouble seeing puns as speakers and may respond to them with a similar irritation.

Everywhere we look for sense, and in language we usually have a good idea in advance of what the nature of that sense is likely to be. In the expectation of a particular sense, we have little difficulty in discarding or being completely unaware of potential nonsense. We may not be able to predict exactly what a writer or speaker is going to say, but we know enough not to consider unlikely alternatives. If we know so little of what others are talking about that we can make no predictions of what they are likely to say, it won't be possible for us to comprehend them in any case.

Meaning always has priority. Begin to read a book or magazine article to a friend, then stop suddenly and ask for a repetition of what you have just said. You will probably find that your listener's short-term memory is not filled with the exact words you have just read, but that you will be given back a similar meaning to what you have said in more or less the same words. It is easy to show that children also pay more attention to meaning than to actual words. Try to correct a child who says, "I ain't got no candy," by asking him to say, "I haven't any candy," and he is likely to repeat "I ain't got no candy" until one of you quits through exasperation. If you appeal, "Can't you even hear what I'm saying?" the answer probably would have to be no—in a literal sense. The child doesn't hear the surface structure of your words but rather perceives a meaning that is returned to you in the child's own words.

Sense-seeking children find literal imitation so difficult—particularly when the language they are expected to copy is not their own—that it may take them a long time to realize that someone might want them to engage in the nonsensical task of repeating sounds. There is no sense in surface structure. A child who reads "John didn't have no candy" when the text is that John had no candy may well be reading more efficiently than a child who identifies each word correctly.

Stated baldly, the assertion that the comprehension of language is not the converse of its production—that readers don't derive meaning from print by an opposite process to that of the writer who put the meaning there originally—may sound too facile. From where do we get this special skill that enables us to comprehend language by bringing sense to what we are about to hear or read in the immediate future? The next chapter will examine how the generation and testing of predictions is the way we comprehend everything in life. Language doesn't require a special skill in order to be understood. Rather, it draws upon a general ability that every individual exhibits from the first weeks of life. Prediction is not a new and artificial skill that has to be learned, but the natural way to make sense of the world.

SUMMARY

Nonvisual information is critically important in reading because meaning is not directly represented in the surface structure of language, in the sounds of speech, or in the visible marks of writing. Readers must bring meaning—deep structure—to what they read, employing their prior knowledge of the topic and of the language of the text. Once again, this use of nonvisual information is impossible if the material being read doesn't make sense to the reader.

CHAPTER 7

Constructing a Theory of the World

So far I have considered the human brain mainly in terms of restrictions, for example, the constant risk of tunnel vision in the face of large amounts of visual information and the limited capacity of short-term memory. I have also tried to show that the way in which we perceive the world is largely determined by what we know and expect, and that we naturally overcome the brain's limited capacity to handle new information by making maximum use of everything we already know. Now I must talk more explicitly about what it is that "we already know" and how we use it. I shall examine—from a psychological point of view—what it is that we carry around all the time in our head. What we already have in our head is our only resource for both making sense of the world and learning more about it.

What is it that we have in our head, that we carry around with us all the time in order to make sense of the world? It's not sufficient to answer "memories," because the human brain is not like a souvenir album filled with an assortment of images and records of past events. At the very least we would have to say that the brain contains memories-with-a-meaning; our memories are related to everything else that we know. But it is also not sufficient to say that our heads are filled with knowledge, in the sense of an accumulation of facts and figures; the brain is not like an encyclopedia or catalog or even like a library, where useful information is filed away under appropriate headings for ready reference. It is not a "database." Certainly the human brain is not a vault in which the fruits of instruction are deposited when and if we attend to our teachers and our textbooks. Instead, what we have in the human brain is an intricately organized and internally consistent model of the world, built up as a result of experience—not instruction—and integrated into a coherent whole as a result of continual effortless learning and thought. We know far more than we were ever taught.

What we have in our head is a theory of what the world is like, and this theory is the basis of all our perception and understanding of the world; it is the root of all learning, the source of all hopes and fears, motives and expectations, reasoning and creativity. This theory is all we have; there is nothing else. If we can make sense of the world at all, it is by interpreting events in the world with respect to our theory. If we can learn at all, it is by modifying and elaborating our theory. Our imagination takes wings from the flight deck of our theory.

RELATING THE PRESENT TO THE PAST

I use the term *theory* deliberately because the theory of the world that we have in our head functions in exactly the same ways as a theory in science, and for exactly the same reasons. The main reasons why a theory is a scientific necessity can conveniently be summarized under the headings of *past, present,* and *future.*

The first reason that scientists must have theories is in order to summarize their *past* experience. Scientists aren't interested in data; heaps of data merely clutter up their computers and interfere with the running of further experiments. Scientists instead strive for the best summary of their data, for statements of the regularities and invariances that seem to underlie experimental events, integrating the present with the past. Scientists don't want to remember that on 15 specific occasions the mixture of liquid A with powder B was followed by explosion C. Instead they want a rule, a summary, that the mixture of liquid A with powder B produces explosion C. Theories are integrated collections of such summary rules.

In a far more general sense, our brain doesn't want to remember that on November 15 we sat on a chair, that on November 16 we sat on a chair, that on November 17 we sat on a chair, and so forth. What the brain wants to remember is that chairs are for sitting on, a summary of experience. Everything we know about chairs, and about tables and houses and cars, about different kinds of food, about different people's roles, about what can be done and everything that happens and everything that isn't likely to happen in the world is a summary of experience, either direct or acquired through observation or communication. Generally we remember specific events only when they are exceptions to our summary rules, or when they have a particularly dramatic or powerful or emotional significance for us. Everything we understand about the world is a summary of our experience, and specific memories that can't be related to our summary, to our general rules, will make no sense to us.

The brain seems so concerned with summarizing experience that it usually doesn't bother to memorize details of anything it already knows in general. We can't remember specifically what we had for breakfast yesterday morning because it was probably no different from what we have for breakfast every morning. But if we had eaten something unusual for breakfast, then we would have remembered it easily today.

The second reason that scientists must have theories is to make sense of the world they are in at *present*, to interpret new data coming in. Events that scientists can't relate to their theories just don't make sense to them; theories protect scientists from bewilderment. And it is for such protection that we all need a theory embracing all of the world as we perceive it.

As I look around my world, I distinguish a multiplicity of meaningful objects that have all kinds of complicated relations to each other and to me. But none of these objects or interrelations is self-evident. A chair doesn't announce itself to me as a chair; I have to recognize it as such. A chair doesn't tell me that I can sit on it, or put my coat or books or feet on it, or stand on it to reach a high shelf, or wedge it against a door I don't wish to be opened. All the order and complexity I see in the world must reflect an order and complexity that exists in my head. I can only make sense of the world in terms of what I already know. Anything I couldn't relate to what I already know—to my theory of the world—would not make sense to me. I would be bewildered.

When was the last time you were bewildered? The very fact that bewilderment is such a rare condition for most of us, despite the complexity of our lives, indicates that our theory of the world is at least as complex as the world as we perceive it. The reason we aren't usually aware of the theory is simply that it works so well. Just as a fish takes water for granted until deprived of it, so we become aware of our dependence on a theory to make sense of the world only when the theory proves inadequate, when the world fails to make sense. When were you last bewildered by something that you heard or read? Our theory of the world seems ready to make sense of almost everything we are likely to experience in spoken and written language. A powerful theory indeed!

And yet, when was the last time you saw a bewildered baby? Infants have theories, too—not as complex as those of adults, but, then, they haven't had as much time to make their theories complex. Children's theories work very well for the worlds they live in. Even the smallest children rarely seem confused or uncertain. The first time many children may run into a situation they can't possibly relate to anything they already know, when they are consistently bewildered, is when they arrive at school.

PREDICTION—THE THEORY IN THE FUTURE

Our personal theory of the world, our summary of past experience, is more than a means of making sense of the present. Our theory is the arena of all our thought. The sober discipline of logical reasoning and the most exuberant flights of creative imagination all take place within its bounds. Scientists use their theories to make hypotheses that are the basis of future experiments, and our personal theory of the world is similarly employed to anticipate coming events. The third function of the theory is to predict the *future.*

Our lives would be impossible, we would be afraid even to leave our beds in the morning, if we had no expectation about what each day might bring. We would be reluctant to walk out of a room if we could make no prediction about what might happen on the other side of the door. We live in a constant state of anticipation, but once again we are generally unaware of this because our theory functions so efficiently. When our predictions fail, we are surprised.

We drive through a town we have never visited before, yet nothing we see surprises us. There is nothing surprising about the buses and cars and pedestrians we see on the main street; they are predictable. But we didn't predict that we might see anything; we would have been surprised to see camels or submarines in the main street. Not that there is anything very surprising or unpredictable about camels or submarines in themselves—we would not have been surprised to see camels if we had been visiting a zoo or to see submarines at a naval base. In other words, our predictions are very specific to situations. We don't predict that anything will happen, nor do we predict that something is bound to happen if it is only *likely* to happen (we are no more surprised by the absence of a bus than we are by the presence of one), but we do predict that many things are unlikely to happen. Our predictions are remarkably precise, but once again that can only be because our theory of the world is remarkably efficient—so much so that when our predictions fail, we are surprised. When was the last time you were surprised?

But, then, when was the last time you saw a baby who was surprised? It isn't easy to surprise a baby. (I don't mean to *startle* a baby, with a sudden shock, but to present an infant with a situation that is unexpected, unpredicted.) It is possible to surprise infants, but sometimes it takes a little ingenuity. Wave a rough papier-mâché mask of a human face—just a schematic nose with an eye on either side and a mouth beneath—in front of 6-month-old babies and they won't give it a second look: *Ho hum, we've seen things like that before.* At 6 months infants aren't surprised by the appearance of a human face. But show the same infants the same papier-mâché face but with both eyes on the same side of the nose, and this time the infants will show all the symptoms of surprise. This is something they did not predict. Their response is not dissimilar to that of adults the first time they meet a portrait by Picasso.

THE NEED FOR PREDICTION

Why should we predict? Why shouldn't we expect that anything might happen and thus free ourselves from any possibility of surprise? I can think of three reasons. The first reason is that in the changing world in which we live, we are usually far more concerned with what is likely to happen in the near and distant future than we are with what is happening right now. We sometimes want to predict the future so that we can prevent or prepare for it.

Every time we drive a car we are taking a trip through the future. We are never concerned with where the car is now (unless it happens to be stationary) but with where it will be at various times in the future. I want to predict whether that truck at the intersection is likely to cross my path some time before it actually hits me. I must decide if my car and that pedestrian ahead will be trying to share the same spot on the road at the same time in the future. An important difference between a skilled driver and a learner is that the skilled driver is able to project the car into the future while the learner's mind is more closely anchored to where the car is now—when it is usually too late to avoid accidents. The same difference tends to distinguish skilled readers from beginners, or from anyone having difficulty with a particular piece of reading. In fluent reading the eye is always ahead of the words the brain is actually working on, checking for possible obstacles to a particular understanding. (This phenomenon is most easily demonstrated if the light is suddenly put out or the book closed while you are reading aloud. You continue reading a few words after you can no longer see, a clear indication that your eyes were ahead of your voice.) Readers concerned with the word directly in front of their nose are having trouble predicting, and they will be likely to suffer tunnel vision.

The second reason for prediction is that there is too much ambiguity in the world, too many ways of interpreting just about anything that confronts us. Unless we exclude some alternatives in advance, we are likely to be overwhelmed with possibilities. The object that I see in front of me may be a chair, but if I'm looking for somewhere to put my coat I don't want to be concerned with the fact that a chair is for sitting on or that it generally has four legs. What I see is related to what I'm looking for, not to all the possibilities. I know where milk comes from, but that is not what I want to think of when I need a cool drink. Some authorities on language say that the meaning of a word is everything it makes us think of, but that obviously doesn't apply to real life. The word *table* has many meanings, but there is only one meaning that I'm concerned with, that I predict, if someone tells me to put my books on the table. As I explained in the previous chapter, all the everyday words of our language have many meanings and often alternative grammatical functions, but in predicting the possible meanings a word is likely to have on a particular occasion, we're just not aware of the potential ambiguities.

The final reason for prediction is that there would otherwise be far too many alternatives to choose among. As I showed in Chapter 4, the brain requires time to make its decisions about what the eyes are looking at, and the time that it requires depends on the number of alternatives. It takes much longer to decide that we are looking at the letter A when it could be any one of the 26 letters of the alphabet than when we know that it is a vowel or that it is either A or B.

Now I can give a more specific explanation of what I have meant all this time by "prediction": *prediction is the prior elimination of unlikely alternatives.* Prediction isn't reckless guessing, nor is it a matter of taking a chance by betting on the most likely outcome. We don't go through life saying "Around the next corner I shall see a bus" or "The next word I read will be *rhinoceros.*" We predict by disregarding unlikely alternatives. We use our theory of the world to tell us the most probable occurrences and leave the brain to decide among those remaining alternatives until our uncertainty is reduced to zero. And we are so good at predicting only the most likely alternatives that we are rarely surprised.

Put more informally, prediction is a matter of asking questions. We don't look out of the window and wonder, "What shall I see?"; we ask, "Shall I see buses or cars or pedestrians?" and provided that what we are looking at falls within that limited range of alternatives, our perception is effortless, efficient, and unsurprised. I don't ask, "What is that object over there, and what can it be used for?" but "Can I put my books on it?" or whatever I want to do. We don't look at a page of print with no expectation about what we shall read next; instead we ask, "What is the hero going to do? Where is the villain going to hide? and Will there be an explosion when liquid A is mixed with powder B?" And provided the answer lies within the expected range of alternatives—which it usually does if we are reading with comprehension—then we aren't aware of any doubt or ambiguity.

THE RELATIVITY OF COMPREHENSION

Now at last I can say what I mean by *comprehension* (or *understanding*). *Prediction* is asking questions, and *comprehension* is getting these questions answered. As we read, as we listen to a speaker, as we go through life, we are constantly asking questions, and as long as these questions are answered, as long as we are left with no residual uncertainty, we comprehend. We don't comprehend how to repair an appliance if we can't answer our own question, "Which of these parts goes where?" We don't comprehend speakers of a foreign language if we can't answer questions like "What are they trying to tell me?" And we don't comprehend a book or newspaper article if we can't find answers that we believe reside in the print.

You may observe that such a definition of comprehension is different from the way the word is used in school. Teachers often regard comprehension as the result of learning rather than the basis for making sense of anything. So-called comprehension tests are usually given after a book has been read and, as a consequence, are more like tests of long-term memory. The fact that teachers sometimes ask how to measure comprehension illustrates the confusion. Comprehension is not a quantity, it is a state—a state of not having any unanswered questions.

Because comprehension is a state of zero uncertainty, there is, in the end, only one person who can say whether an individual comprehends something or not, and that is that particular individual. A test can't tell me that I really did understand a book or a speaker if my feeling is that I did not. Of course there are some obvious clues that will indicate whether a person is failing to comprehend. If my eyes glaze over while you talk or my brow furrows deeply as I read, these are reasonable hints that all is not well with my comprehension. But the ultimate test must lie within the individual. This is the contention that so many teachers find so difficult to accept—that the best way of determining whether children can make sense of a book or a lesson from their own point of view is not to give them a test, but simply to ask, "Did you understand?" (A child who will dissimulate is not making reading a meaningful activity in any case.)

The very notion that comprehension is relative, that it depends on the questions that an individual happens to ask, is not one that all teachers are happy with. They want to argue that you may not have understood a book however little uncertainty you are left with at the end. They will ask, "But did you see that the police officer's failure to catch the speeding motorcyclist was really a symbol of ineluctable human helplessness in the face of manifest destiny?" If you say, "No, I just thought it was a jolly good story," they will tell you that you didn't really comprehend what the story was about. But basically what they are saying is that you weren't asking the kind of question they think you should have asked while reading the book, and that is another matter altogether. If there are particular questions a teacher thinks a student should ask, then the teacher should announce them before the book is read, so that the student can truly predict and look for answers. But the teacher should be careful. Once again, too many questions, especially if the student doesn't really understand their point, can destroy comprehension altogether. (Sometimes a teacher will object, "If I tell students the questions in advance, they won't read any other part of the book." But isn't that what any intelligent person would do? When we look up a telephone number, do we read and try to memorize every other name and number in the directory?)

To reiterate: The basis of comprehension is prediction, and prediction is achieved by making use of what we already know about the world, by making use of our theory of the world. There is no need to teach children to predict; it is a natural activity, and they have been doing it since they were born. Prediction is a natural part of living.

Without it we would have been overcome by the world's uncertainty and ambiguity long before we arrived at school.

There is also no need to instruct a child on the need to develop a theory of the world; this also is a normal part of being alive and growing up. From their earliest days infants summarize their past in order to make sense of the present and to predict the future. Without such a theory they would be constantly bewildered and frequently surprised. And neither bewilderment nor surprise is a condition that anyone is willing to tolerate for very long. It is a natural propensity of children to make their theories as extensive and efficient as possible.

How extensive is our theory of the world? To catalog this theory would be to catalog the world as we perceive it. All the order and complexity and predictability we detect in the world must reflect an order and complexity and ability to predict within our own brains. Of course, children's theories aren't as complex as adults'—but no one's theory is ever complete. Perhaps I can distinguish more kinds of tree than you, although your theory is richer for distinguishing moths from butterflies, or for repairing car engines. The fact that a child may not be able to distinguish cats from dogs or the letter A from the letter B doesn't necessarily entail confusion or bewilderment, any more than I'm usually confused or bewildered by my inability to distinguish moths from butterflies. These are just problems we haven't yet got around to solving. A child's theory may be less differentiated than yours, but until you see a child who is constantly bewildered or surprised—and not just by what goes on in school, but by every aspect of life in general—you can't say that the child doesn't know how to predict or to make sense of the world. Children know how to comprehend, provided they are in a situation that has the possibility of making sense to them.

SUMMARY

The foundation of comprehension is the theory of the world that we all have constructed and carry around with us all the time. This theory is constantly tested and modified in all our interactions with the world. It is the source of the predictions that enable us to make sense of events and of language. We can't make sense of the world—or of reading—if the situation confronting us can't be related to our theory of the world, if it is nonsense.

CHAPTER 8

Letters, Words, and Meaning

So far I have talked very broadly about how the eyes and brain work, about the functions of memory and the nature of language, about how we predict in order to comprehend and how we hypothesize and experiment in order to learn. These excursions were required before we could come back to our central topic of reading because they all lie at the roots of reading. As I have said from the beginning, there is nothing unique about the act of reading; to understand reading it is necessary to understand more general topics. But now that we are at the threshold of a detailed discussion of reading, there is a consolation: There is little that is new to be added. Much of what I shall now say about reading will pull together what I have said so far.

If we examine first the particular abilities that fluent readers demonstrate, then we shall have a basis for considering what beginning readers must learn to do. This will help us to avoid the fallacy of confusing the nature of reading with the way reading is taught. One reason for the conventional oversimplification that reading is primarily the decoding of letters to sound must be that "learning the sounds of letters" is what many of us mistakenly believe made us readers. What teachers actually accomplish may be very different from what they think they are doing. While trying to explain the sounds of letters, for example, they often read with their students and provide experience of the recognition of words and the comprehension of meaning. So in addition to analyzing reading before considering learning to read, we must separate learning to read from all the rituals of teaching reading.

The present chapter is fairly technical, concerned with the way readers identify letters, words, and meaning. Earlier chapters have taken a wider view of reading in all its richness, in the ways in which it permeates our lives. The link between these chapters is that the basis of all reading, like every other aspect of comprehension, is asking questions. Whether we read to identify letters, words, or meanings depends on what we are looking for, and the way we make sense of different reading situations, from consulting telephone directories to immersing ourselves in novels, depends on what we expect to find.

Despite the widespread belief that readers need to recognize letters in order to identify words—and words, to comprehend meaning—reading actually works in the reverse direction. Normally we need to understand meaning in order to identify words, and normally we try to identify words in order to identify letters. In fact we don't usually bother to go down the scale at all—we ignore letters if our aim is to identify words, and we ignore words if we are reading to make sense. To explain all these rather unfamiliar ideas I must go one step at a time—in the reverse order—discussing first how readers identify letters.

THE IDENTIFICATION OF LETTERS

Here is a simple question: What is the letter in the box below?

K

Here is a difficult question: How did you know? You can't answer that you learned long ago that the letter was called "K" because that would beg the question. I didn't ask how you knew its name, but how you recognized in the first place the letter that you are calling "K." Before you can put a name to anything you must recognize it, you must "know what it looks like." What is it you know that enables you to recognize a letter of the alphabet? This is indeed a difficult question. Scientists who study the visual system are quite uncertain about what precisely goes on when the eye and brain effortlessly perform their daily business of recognizing all the thousands of objects and shapes that are familiar to us. But it seems reasonably clear that the task isn't accomplished by committing specific "images" of what we want to recognize to memory. We don't have a picture book or files of letter shapes in the brain to which we refer whenever we want to say what a letter is. You didn't recognize the K in the box by comparing it with a set of conveniently labeled pictures or representations of the alphabet in the mind.

One reason it is unlikely that we learn to recognize the alphabet by memorizing the shapes of letters is that letters come in so many shapes and sizes:

k K k k k K K k k k K K K k K k

There were probably one or two K's in the previous sequence that you had never seen before in that identical form and that were therefore different from any "picture" you might have in your memory. The situation is quite general; we can identify cats and dogs we have never previously seen, just as we can recognize faces and cars from angles at which we have never seen them before.

We may not have given much thought to the question of how letters of the alphabet—or cats, dogs, people, and cars—are recognized, and the question of how we do so may itself sound a bit odd. But our lack of curiosity is because we are so good at recognizing familiar objects and forms. Visual recognition is one of those incredibly complex skills for which we give the brain little credit because both the learning and the performance of the skills are usually accomplished without strain or awareness. But it is important for anyone concerned with reading to understand that we don't learn to recognize letters or anything else simply by "memorizing" shapes, even if many views about how reading should be taught seem to be based on just that assumption.

The simplest answer to the question of how you were able to recognize the letter K in the previous example is that you decided it couldn't be one of the other 25 letters of the alphabet. In other words, what you have learned is how to distinguish each letter of the alphabet from all the others. You have knowledge about what constitutes significant differences among the letters of the alphabet.

(Perhaps you can begin to see why different views of how letters are learned make a difference to reading instruction. A "picture-memorizing" view might suggest that a child should be taught letters of the alphabet one at a time, given lots of practice until A is learned, and then move on to B, and so forth. But the view I am now outlining suggests that in order to learn how to identify any letter, you must see what the alternatives are. Children can't even begin to learn to recognize A until they can compare it with every letter that is not A.)

The important word in the explanation that letters are recognized on the basis of significant differences is *significant.* Some differences make a difference and others don't, depending always on circumstances. There are differences between k and K—the two letters clearly don't look absolutely alike—but these differences aren't usually significant to readers because we normally want to treat the two letters as the same, namely as "k." The letters K and H also don't look alike, but this time there must be differences that are significant because the two letters can't be treated as if they are the same. So the problem for anyone learning to distinguish K from H is to discover the differences that are *significant,* the differences that make a difference.

DISTINCTIVE FEATURES

Researchers sometimes refer to these significant differences as *distinctive features.* Presumably one of the distinctive features of A, for example, as compared with H, is that it comes to a point on top (or that it is "closed" at the top rather than "open"). A distinctive feature of O compared with C must have something to do with the closure of a circle. However, it's not possible to be specific about what actually constitutes the set of distinctive features of letters (or of anything else) for the very good reason that we don't know enough in detail about how the visual system works. Scientists can't say precisely what the eye looks for. And in any case, another good reason for not speculating too much about distinctive features is that some teachers might be tempted to try to teach these features to children, a concern that is certainly unnecessary and possibly distracting.

Incidentally, learning to make distinctions on the basis of significant differences among alternatives is, again, not a process unique to reading; it applies naturally to everything else we can distinguish, including cats and dogs. We are able to identify a cat at a glance from the other side of the street, even when it is a cat that we have never seen before, because we have knowledge that enables us to distinguish cats from dogs and from other four-legged animals that aren't cats. Having four legs isn't a distinctive feature of cats compared with dogs, although it is, of course, a distinctive feature of both cats and dogs when compared with snakes and goldfish.

Two points emerge from the analogy of cat and dog recognition for recognition of letters of the alphabet. The first is that we aren't usually aware of all the distinctive features that enable us to distinguish different things. The knowledge is implicit—we clearly have it in our brains, but it isn't knowledge that we can put into words. The second point is that what constitutes a distinctive feature is relative to the distinctions we want to make. What enables us to distinguish a dog from a cat may not enable us to distinguish a dog from a wolf.

To say that our ability to recognize individual letters is based on a knowledge of distinctive features rather than on an internalized set of pictures is another way of saying that we have learned rules, or procedures, for distinguishing letters of the alphabet. We have acquired a set of rules that enable us to test whether a particular letter is K or some other letter of the alphabet. We shall soon be very concerned with how these rules are learned, but for the moment I want to illustrate the way we employ rules or distinctive features to distinguish letters. The discussion will bring together a lot of the research evidence I alluded to earlier in the book and will provide a basis for explaining how we can recognize words and comprehend meanings so fluently.

There are several lines of evidence supporting the distinctive-feature view; for example, the fact that even if we can't obtain enough visual information to identify a letter for certain, we can often have a good idea of what the letter is not. We may confuse the letter *a* with *e* or *s* but never with *k*, while *m* might be confused with *w* but not with *p*. This suggests that even a glimpse of part of a letter—discrimination of a few distinctive features—can help eliminate some alternatives.

The ease with which we can identify any letter depends on the number of alternatives that we think the letter might be. It is easier to recognize A if we know in advance that it is a vowel than if we think it could be any one of the 26 letters of the alphabet. We can recognize the letter more quickly, or when it is smaller or further away, with less chance of error. This fact—that ease of recognition doesn't depend simply on how big or clearly printed the letter is but also on the uncertainty of the reader—is based on a wealth of experimental evidence; nevertheless, it comes as something of a surprise. Common sense might tell us that either we can see a letter or we can't, just as common sense might tell us that either we have learned to recognize a letter or we have not. But, in fact, the ease with which we can both learn and identify a letter depends on the number of alternatives. The fewer the alternatives, the less evidence we need to make a decision. This is a universal phenomenon, as I pointed out when talking about perception and comprehension generally. The evidence you require to identify a letter—the number of distinctive features you need to discriminate—depends on how many different letters you think it could possibly be.

This fact that individual letters can be recognized in a poorer light, or from a greater distance, if some limitation is placed on the number of alternatives that the letter might be, can only be explained by the distinctive-feature theory. If letter recognition were a matter of matching a shape with a picture in the head, what would it matter if there were two alternatives or 200? Either you would see a letter or you wouldn't, and clues would not help. The distinctive-feature theory helps to account for the important demonstration we considered at some length in Chapter 4, when we saw that in one second of reading the visual system could deal with only four or five letters if the letters were selected at random:

> W K H M Y

but twice as many if the letters were arranged into words:

> FURY HORSES

When letters are printed at random, the probability of each letter is 1 in 26 and a good deal of distinctive-feature information is required to make a decision. But when letters are organized into words, the relative probability of each letter is reduced to an average of about 1 in 8. (If you see the letter Q in an English word, you need not discriminate any distinctive features to tell you what the next letter will be. Furthermore, after QU there are only four alternatives.)

I also talked in Chapter 4 about the trade-off between visual and nonvisual information in reading, explaining that the more nonvisual information you have behind the eyes, the less visual information from the page your brain has to handle. It is the nonvisual information, or what you already know about how letters occur in words, that reduces alternatives for you in advance. The distinctive features available in the letters on the page constitute the visual information that enables you to decide among the remaining alternatives. You wouldn't be able to make use of your prior knowledge in order to identify in a single glance two or more times as many letters when they occur in predictable sequences unless you were able to make use of the identification of units of information much smaller than a single letter—of distinctive features, in other words.

This explanation, incidentally, should now help you realize that the test I gave when I asked if you could identify the K in the box was the most difficult I could devise without making the actual letter more difficult to discriminate. I could have made the task much easier by telling you that the letter was in the first half of the alphabet, or that it was either J, K, L, or M, for example. Of course, we aren't usually aware of the gain in time or clarity when the number of alternatives that a letter might be is reduced, but that is because in situations of the kind I have described we normally have more than enough time and information to make our decision. It is only on the rare occasions when we might be called on to read through lists of random letters rapidly—or if we are schoolchildren required to identify what is to them nonsense on a board, book, or computer monitor—that the difficulty of identifying letters on the basis of visual information alone can make itself evident.

Here is also evidence that reading is not a passive activity that begins with the print on the page and ends with a reaction in the brain. Even as simple a matter as recognizing letters of the alphabet begins with a question that we are asking—the predicted range of alternatives—and ends with a search for an answer on the page. The question is always in terms of the alternatives we are considering. Sometimes we can look at exactly the same distinctive features and get quite different answers, depending on the question we happen to be asking. If we are asking a question about letters, then the features in IO will be read as letters, as in the word LION. But if our question is about numbers, then the same features will give us a numerical answer, as in the sequence 210.

THE IDENTIFICATION OF WORDS

Here is another easy question: What is the word in the box?

HOUSE

Here is another difficult question: How did you know? As I explained at the beginning of Chapter 3, you certainly didn't recognize the word by sounding it out—by putting together the sounds of individual letters. If I had timed you, we would have found that it takes little longer to put a name to the entire word than to utter the name (or sound) of a single letter. Besides, I'm sure you didn't run through the 11 different ways of pronouncing HO before you said what the word was. Nor did you recognize the word on the basis of its spelling—you didn't read the letters H-O-U-S-E and refer to some kind of internal dictionary to ascertain that those letters spelled the word *house*. If you could read the word *house* at all, then, you would have recognized it at once, without working it out through phonics or spelling. You would have recognized the word as a unit, just as you earlier recognized the letter K as a unit, and indeed just as you would recognize a real house or a picture of a house as a unit, not a bit at a time. In other words, when we read a word we don't read individual letters at all.

In many written languages, of course, there are no letters to be recognized. Chinese children learn that 家 is the written symbol for *house*—they can't sound it out. For fluent readers of English like you and me, the fact that the words of our written language are made up of letters is largely irrelevant—we recognize words in the same way that fluent Chinese readers recognize the words of their nonalphabetic written language, as self-contained and immediately recognizable units.

In Chapter 3, you may recall, I made a distinction between two aspects of learning to identify words: finding out the "name" of the word and remembering how to recognize on future occasions the printed marks to which the name should be attached. Phonics was only one way—a relatively inefficient way—of finding out the name of unfamiliar words and had nothing to do with the way words are normally recognized. Now we can examine further how words are recognized so that their names and possible meanings can be related to visual information. The answer is that words are recognized in exactly the same way that cats, dogs, cars, faces, and letters of the alphabet are recognized. Words are recognized on the basis of significant differences among alternatives, on the basis of distinctive features.

We learn to recognize words by learning to distinguish them from each other. Exactly the same arguments apply to the recognition of words that I have just used to support the distinctive-feature theory for the recognition of letters. Asking you—or a child—to recognize a word in isolation is the hardest word-recognition task that can be given. The word *house* would have been much easier for you to recognize—and you would have been more confident that you were right—if I had told you that it was a type of building or if I had put it into a sentence. When words are in a meaningful context, or when we already have a good idea of what they are likely to be, we can see them much quicker and over a much greater distance than if we have no prior expectations at all.

As with letters, so with words. It isn't simply a case of either we see a word or we don't, any more than it is a case of either we have learned a word or we haven't. The ease with which we recognize words depends on the number of alternatives we think there are. The more alternatives, the more information or distinctive features we need to discriminate. In a meaningful sequence like *I like e _ _ s and b _ _ _ n for breakfast*, we need to see only small parts of a word to be able to recognize it. And these small parts aren't whole letters, either; the distinctive features of words are clearly smaller than letters because an entire word can be recognized in the time it takes to identify a single letter. Obviously we don't spend as much time on any of the letters in a word as we would spend on the letters in isolation. Letters can be mutilated so much that it is impossible to identity them by themselves, yet they are recognizable in words.

The fact that the number of distinctive features required to identify a word depends on the number of alternatives helps to explain another aspect of the Chapter 4 demonstration that I have already discussed. We can see only two unrelated words—like FURY HORSES—if each word could be one of many thousands of alternatives. But when the number of alternatives is limited, because the words are grammatical and make sense, we can see twice as much—EARLY FROSTS HARM THE CROPS.

What are the distinctive features of words? Obviously they include many of the distinctive features of letters since words are made up of letters, with perhaps one or two additional features like relative length of the word and the relative position of the letter in the word. If you know a word is either *cat* or *cucumber*, length alone will identify it for you. The distinctive features of words, like the distinctive features of letters, must lie in the printed marks on the page or screen. Sometimes—when we want to identify letters—we look at those marks, the "visual information" of print, and see letters. Sometimes—when we want to identify words—we look at the same marks and see words.

In other words, whether we see letters or words depends on the question we are asking. The answer always lies in the same source of information, the distinctive features in the ink marks on the page. Similarly, whether we see IO as numbers or letters depends on what we expect.

We can see letters without seeing words, as you would if I asked you to read the letters in the word *house* backwards. But we can also see words without seeing letters. You don't have to read H-O-U-S-E in order to read the word *house*. In fact it isn't possible to do the two things at the same time; you can't see both letters and words in the same place at the same time, any more than you can see the two faces and the vase at the same time in the following illustration.

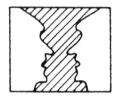

The brain can only handle the answer to one question at a time. Attention to the meaning of words, for example, can make you oblivious to their spelling, as any proofreader knows.

Now perhaps you can see why I wanted to talk about letter recognition before talking about word recognition—because it is simpler to explain the notion of distinctive features with reference to letters. But now I hope you also see why I stressed that I was putting letter recognition first simply for convenience, and that I didn't want you to think that letter recognition was a necessary prerequisite for word recognition, either in learning or performing the recognition skill. When you recognize words that are familiar to you, you need pay no attention to letters at all. We only attend to letters when we fail to recognize whole words, and unless we have a fairly reasonable idea of what a word might be, using the letters to sound it out will do little to help. As I have already pointed out, there are easier ways of identifying unfamiliar words.

MAKING SENSE OF WRITTEN LANGUAGE

The idea that both letters and words are recognized in the same way, through the discrimination of distinctive features that are elements of written language smaller even than a letter, doesn't usually cause too much difficulty. Although our immediate intuitions may be to the contrary, it isn't hard to grasp that if individual letters are recognized on the basis of distinctive features, then words themselves should be distinguishable from each other by virtue of the same features, without the intervening necessity to identify letters. But the next step will probably be a little harder to grasp. When we identify meaning in text, it is not necessary to identify individual words. We can make sense of text directly from the distinctive features of the print, from those same distinctive features in the ink marks on the page that we can employ for the recognition of letters and words.

We may think we see words we read, but there are several reasons for this misconception. For a start, this is a case where we can't trust our own senses. The mere circumstance of wondering whether we identify words when we read will ensure that we are indeed aware of recognizing words as we read, at least for as long as we ask ourselves that question. It is impossible to observe oneself reading to see if we are aware of words without in fact being aware of words (just as we may think we "subvocalize," or articulate words silently to ourselves, every time we read because whenever we listen for this inner voice we are bound to subvocalize). But the fact that we can't avoid focusing our attention on words if we look to see if we are attending to words doesn't mean that we normally read by identifying words. It would be impossible to read normally—that is, to make sense of the print—and at the same time attend to the individual words.

Perhaps at some point during the last few sentences you indeed wondered if you were aware of individual words as you read. And if for a while you became aware of words, then at least one and probably both of the following things happened to you: You slowed down in order to read-one-word-at-a-time and for a while you lost track of meaning. I don't want to assert that you can't recognize individual words when you read; obviously you can. But the recognition of individual words is not necessary for comprehension; it can interfere with comprehension, and conversely, comprehension is often necessary if you want to identify individual words.

The fact that words are so obviously there on the page in front of us is no justification for asserting that we attend to them as words, any more than the fact that words are made up of letters entails that we identify every letter. Obviously we look at words, in the same sense that we look at the paper they are printed on, but we need be no more aware of the words than we are of the paper if we are concerned with meaning. The moment we pay attention to such irrelevant details as the paper or the print, we risk losing focus on the sense of what we are reading.

The matter is further complicated because letters and words—or their surface structures—are so self-evident, but the very notion of a "meaning" is vague and intangible. You can't point to a particular unit of written language and say, "There is one meaning," in the same way that you can point and say, "There is one word," or, "There is one letter." Furthermore, there is the weight of so much conventional opinion for the opposite point of view. The response of many teachers when they first grasp the implications of what I'm about to explain is, "Why were we never told this before, in our training?"

At the moment I want to present the evidence that the apprehension of meaning can precede the identification of individual words, and then try to show that reading normally demands comprehension prior to and even without the identification of words. These may be difficult ideas to grasp, but they are crucial.

The technique generally employed by researchers to demonstrate the preeminence of meaning is to show that sequences of words are identified faster if they are meaningful than if they are not. For an example, we can turn once again to the demonstration in Chapter 4 that two unrelated words could be read in a single glance:

> FURY HORSES

but that more than twice as many can be read in the same time if the words make sense:

> EARLY FROSTS HARM THE CROPS

The argument is that the second sequence could not have been identified a word at a time in the same way that FURY HORSES was; otherwise no more than two words of the second sequence would have been identified. Something about the meaningfulness of the entire second sequence facilitated the identification of the individual words; so something about the meaning must have been comprehended before any of the words were identified. And the reason the meaningfulness could have this facilitating effect was also given in Chapter 4: When words are in meaningful sequences, the number of alternatives is very much smaller. The average probability of each word in meaningful sequences is about 1 in 200 rather than 1 in many thousands for isolated, random words.

The facility with which we see a word depends on how many alternatives there are. The fewer alternatives there are, the fewer distinctive features we need to discriminate. Meaningfulness cuts down on the number of alternatives, and thus we are able to make use of meaning to reduce how much we need look at the distinctive features that constitute a word. We can even begin to get clues about the meaning of a phrase before there has been time to identify more than one or two words, as in the example just given. The effect of meaningfulness is extremely powerful. It isn't difficult to demonstrate that it doubles the rate at which we can read, which is another way of saying that the eyes require only half the distinctive-feature information for each word if the words make sense. You can demonstrate this to yourself by seeing how much slower you are at reading a sentence that is written backward: *discriminate to need we features distinctive fewer the, are there alternatives fewer the.*

If you do try to read nonsense at your normal reading speed, you will find you get more words wrong. Not that errors are an unusual occurrence in reading. Despite the emphasis placed on accuracy in school, everyone makes mistakes while reading, even professional readers like actors and broadcasters, unless they rehearse to commit actual words to memory. But the interesting thing about the errors that fluent readers make is that the errors usually make sense—the readers don't read the exact words, but they usually get the meaning right. They might read something like "Johnny hadn't got a ticket" when the text actually says "Johnny had no ticket" but not something like "Johnny had a ticket," which looks more like the text but has a different meaning. Children who are on the way to becoming skillful readers make a lot of mistakes that make sense, reading "Johnny told me . . ." rather than "Johnny said . . . ," suggesting that they have discovered they shouldn't spend too much time looking at particular words. Children who aren't progressing so well tend to look at words more closely and make errors that perhaps are less extreme in terms of visual similarity—"Johnny sand . . ." instead of "Johnny said . . ."—but that make no sense. When they do make a mistake that turns out not to make sense, good readers usually go back and correct themselves, because they are attending to meaning. But children aiming for individual word accuracy may not correct their mistakes, since they are less likely to become aware of them—they aren't following the sense. (Of course, if what the children are reading is nonsense in any case, the good readers will be forced to read just like the bad ones.)

An ingenious demonstration that people read for meaning with complete disregard for the particular words they are looking at has been provided by studies of fluent bilingual adults reading text that switched every couple of words between English and French—like the sentence *His horse, suivi de two dogs, faisait résonner the earth.* Not only could such readers subsequently not remember which parts of the text were in English or French—and some even said they didn't notice that the text was in two languages—but often they read the English words in French or vice versa. They would read, without correcting themselves, English phrases like *two dogs* as *deux chiens,* conserving the meaning, of course, but completely ignoring the actual evidence before their eyes.

Even more dramatic evidence that meaning can be independent of the literal word comes from brain-injured patients who seem to have lost precise word-recognition skills but who can nevertheless grasp the general meaning of familiar words. Some have been reported to have read the word *ill* as *sick, city* as *town,* and *ancient* as *historic.* This phenomenon is not dissimilar to the difficulties of other aphasic patients who can't identify a pair of scissors by name but who can say they are "for cutting." They are able to recognize the sense of something without being able to put an exact name to it.

But, then, there is no good reason to "say" what a written word is, either aloud or silently, in order to grasp its meaning. We get the meaning of *house,* for example, directly from the printed marks and then, if necessary, say the word, just as we recognize a real house before we say, "There is a house." We recognize a face—we comprehend its "meaning" to us—before we put a name to it. Why should it be surprising that we can comprehend a written word's meaning before we put a name to the word? We can't even put a name to some words until we know their meaning. (Should *read* be pronounced "reed" or "red"?) And for many other words, like *their* and *there,* saying the word won't give us the meaning, though it is obvious on sight.

A final illustration comes from experiments in which participants are required to read through lists of words in order to identify a particular target, for example, going down a list of 30 or 40 unrelated five-letter words to find the word *maple*. The task isn't unlike looking for a particular name in a telephone directory. In both cases you find that relatively little time is taken in getting to the word you are looking for because you are paying only minimal attention to the words you don't want. You usually can't say very much about the words that you read that were not the word you were looking for because it's not necessary to identify a word to say what it is not. Far fewer distinctive features are required for a decision that a word isn't something than to confirm that it is. None of this is surprising, perhaps, except that in the experimental situation it has been shown that it takes no longer to find the target word when readers are simply told, "It is a kind of tree," than when they are told specifically that the word is *maple*. They can read for the general meaning just as easily as they can for the specific word. The tendency to concentrate on meaning rather than on the specific word can interfere with reading in some circumstances. It takes longer to find the exact word *maple* when it is hidden in a list of other tree names than when it is among words with a variety of different meanings.

Finally, comprehension must precede the identification of individual words for the simple reason, already discussed, that words taken in isolation, or one at a time, are essentially meaningless. You can't tell the part of speech of common words like *chair, table, house, narrow, empty, waste*, let alone their meaning, unless you have some idea of what you are reading about—unless, in other words, comprehension is preceding the actual words.

But if comprehension is necessary before words can be identified, and if the purpose of reading is to make sense of the text, then there is often no point in identifying the individual words at all. Meaningful language is transparent: We look through the words for the meaning beyond.

You may still want to ask, "I understand that we can find meaning in text without identifying words, but what are the distinctive features of meaning?" The answer is that there are no specific distinctive features for meaning because we are not looking for meaning on the page. We are looking for answers to questions we are asking (or predictions we are making). If distinctive features are found compatible with a prediction, then an identification is made—not of a word, but of a meaning. To find meaning, we look for evidence of it.

SUMMARY

Letter identification, word identification, and the comprehension of meaning are independent consequences of asking different kinds of questions of text. Comprehension need not require word identification, which in turn need not require letter identification.

CHAPTER 9

Joining the Club of Readers

Many children can read before they come to school, so obviously formal instruction in reading isn't essential. And these are by no means the most privileged of children. Many come from large families, single-parent homes, and poor neighborhoods, and are not especially favored academically. If they arrived at school unable to read, it would be anticipated that they would have great difficulty doing so. Yet already they can read. What enabled them to get the necessary understanding?

Whether children have become readers before arriving at school or not, they obviously require particular conditions if they are to achieve the insights that reading requires (discussed in Chapter 2). The meaningfulness of written language doesn't make itself immediately apparent to anyone. I have discussed how adept children are at learning, if print is meaningful to them. The question remains concerning the exact nature of the circumstances in which this learning ability is manifested—and of the circumstances when it is not. Where are the seeds of literacy planted? How must they be nurtured? To understand reading, children must become members of a group of written language users; *they must join the club of readers.*

Children can join the club of readers with a single reciprocal act of affiliation. There are no dues to be paid, no entry standards to be met. A mutual acknowledgment of acceptance into a group of people who use written language is all that is required. Children who join the club of readers take it for granted that they will become like the more experienced members of the club; they are the same kind of people. The experienced members of the club take it for granted that the children will be like them; they are the same kind of people. Expectation doesn't guarantee learning, of course, but it makes it possible. Expectation that learning will *not* take place almost inevitably fulfils the prophesy.

The club of readers functions in much the same way as any other special-interest group. Established members are concerned about each other's interests and welfare. In particular, these members occupy themselves with whatever activities the group has formed itself to promote, constantly demonstrating the value and utility of these activities to new members, helping them to participate in these activities themselves when they want, but never forcing their involvement—and never discriminating against them for lacking the understanding or expertise of more practiced members. Differences in ability and in specific interests are taken for granted.

ADVANTAGES OF CLUB MEMBERSHIP

Here are some advantages of membership in the club of readers for children:

- *They see what written language does.* The uses of written language are complex and manifold; written language can probably be employed in support of every human endeavor. The multiplicity of ways in which written language makes sense in our world is demonstrated to children by the "people like them" who already belong to the club.
- *Children are admitted as neophyte members.* No one expects them to read like more experienced members of the club, but no one doubts that they will do so in due course. They aren't labeled. Mistakes are expected, not frowned upon or punished as undesirable behavior.
- *Members help newcomers to become experts.* There is no specific instruction, no special time when the beginners are expected to demonstrate learning. Instead, someone helps children to read what they are trying to read (and to write what they might try to write). The child is told what the sign says, shown where the label indicates the contents, and assisted in preparing the shopping list or in writing the birthday greeting. The help is always relevant, so that children are never confused about what it is for. Formal instruction may on occasion be asked for or offered, but always it is relevant to something the child is trying to do, and always it is under the control of the child.

- *Children are quickly admitted into a full range of club activities, as activities make sense to them and are useful to them.* They are never required to be involved in something they don't understand or that appears to be pointless. Everything that reading can do for other members of the club is revealed to them in the expectation that they, in turn, will make use of reading in the same way. They always have opportunities to find out what written language will do for them, and how to do these things themselves.

- *Most importantly, children learn to identify themselves as members of the club of readers.* They see themselves as readers. We learn and behave like the people we see ourselves as being like. If we belong to a club, then everything pertaining to the club comes to us naturally, as of right. But if we are excluded from the club, or if we exclude ourselves, then we deliberately constrain ourselves from acting like members of the club. We learn not to be like members of the club. Such constraints are all the more potent because they are often unconscious; we don't recognize that we are holding ourselves back.

- *All of the learning takes place without risk.* There are no high-stakes tests, no examinations; no one expects new members to be as adept as each other or to "progress" at the same rate. There are no planned schedules of learning, no curriculum committees, no accountability, no objectives, no prerequisites, no "standards," and nothing is tested except in use.

Research in a number of cultures has shown that many children know much about written language before they get to school or independently of what they are taught in school. They are familiar with many of the uses of written language, in signs, labels, lists, letters, books, magazines, catalogs, computer programs, and television guides. They know what people do with written language, even if they can't do these things themselves. They also have rough ideas about how written language works: that it consists of symbols on lines, that it is laid out in conventional ways, and that there are rules and regularities of spelling. They pretend to read (and to write) in their role-playing games.

Why should children join the club of readers, even before they know a thing about reading themselves? Because they see people around them engaging in meaningful written language activities, and because they see themselves as being like those people and are accepted in such a way.

There is nothing unusual in any of this. It is precisely the way infants learn to talk and to understand spoken language. No one gives babies formal instruction and examinations in how adults use spoken language; few would learn to talk if they were treated in this manner. Instead, almost from the moment of birth they are admitted into a club of spoken language users, of "people like them," who speak in the way the babies in due course are expected to speak. Quickly infants begin to speak in that way, aided by experienced club members who help them to understand what they want to understand and to say what they want to say.

LEARNING BY READING

Some advantages of joining the club of readers are unique. With spoken language you must usually do your learning with club members who are within reach, in range of your sight as well as your hearing. In the club of readers you can learn from people who are far distant in time and space, who may even no longer be living. In the club of readers you can learn from *authors.*

Margaret Spencer has argued that it is the authors of children's stories who most fully teach children how to read. The children follow a familiar or predictable tale, perhaps with another reader's assistance, and the author shows how the story is actually told in written language. In a sense, a child knows what the words are, and the author shows how the words are written. It is tragic, she says, that in the name of "reading instruction" teachers often come between children and authors. Don't ask who these authors are—they are the particular authors that individual children like to read.

Not surprisingly, children who read a lot tend to be very good readers. It's not that they need to be good readers in order to be able to read a lot, but the act of reading brings about the mastery required.

There are many other things that are learned by reading. The range and depth of comprehension increases, both for written and spoken language. Possibly readers learn to think better—certainly they find more to think about. There are dramatic and consistent increases in vocabulary—an important and well-researched finding. Writing ability improves with reading, and so does spelling. Fluent readers do better in all academic subject areas.

I'm not saying that reading automatically produces all these impressive consequences—there is still one other requirement. Readers must always see themselves as members of the relevant club. Learners who don't see themselves as competent writers or spellers are unlikely to learn much about writing or spelling, from reading or from any other source. But learners who don't read aren't going to learn very much about writing or spelling at all. The problem for many students who encounter difficulties is not the things they fail to learn at school but the things they become convinced they can't and won't learn.

Readers can join any club in the world. Many people developed their vocational and personal interests through the characters they became acquainted with in books. For many individuals, their only chance of getting to know people they might want to emulate, who can guide and inspire them, is through reading. Our very identities can be established through the authors that we read and the characters we read about. Every book offers entrance to new worlds.

READING AND WRITING

Because this book is particularly concerned with reading, I have had little to say about writing. But in the current chapter, when the concern is with learning to read, reference to writing is unavoidable. Reading and writing can no more be dealt with separately in learning than they should be in teaching.

I don't usually refer to children joining the club of readers (or the club of writers) as I have done in this chapter, but rather to *joining the literacy club*. Children learn about both reading and writing as they learn the uses of written language. The distinguishable "skills" of reading and writing are relatively superficial aspects of literacy. The insights and understanding that I have been emphasizing about the meaningfulness and manifold utility of written language are basic to both reading and writing. Everything a child learns about reading helps in becoming a writer. Everything learned about writing contributes to reading ability. To keep the two activities separate does more than deprive them of their basic sense; it impoverishes any learning that might take place.

LEARNING TO BECOME A WRITER

There are two diametrically opposed views on how children learn to write, just as there are about how they learn to read.

In reading, one view is that learning is a result of *direct instruction* of detail, no matter how far removed the learning activities are from sense, as with intensive phonics instruction. The opposite point of view is that learners become readers by reading.

In writing also, one view is that learning is a result of *direct instruction* of detail, no matter how far removed the learning activities are from sense. Children, and adults, are expected to become writers by having their attention focused on such topics as spelling, punctuation, handwriting, and even neatness, all things that can easily be observed and regulated. The opposite point of view is that learners become writers by . . . The usual expectation at this point is that I will say "writing"—you learn to read by reading and you learn to write by writing. But that is not the case. Writing is important for learning to write, but not because much is learned by the act of writing itself. Writing is essential because (and if) it helps learners *see themselves as writers*. All the nuts and bolts of writing—including spelling, punctuation, and grammar, but more importantly the subtle style and structure of written discourse, the appropriate organization of sentences and paragraphs, and the appropriate selection of words and tones of voice—are learned through *reading*.

The point deserves emphasis. *You learn to read by reading and you learn to write by reading*. Learners have to join a club, the club of writers, and the most influential members of that club are again authors, the authors of the books (and other written language) that the fledgling members read.

First, I'll discuss briefly why you can't learn much about writing from instruction, textbooks, and exercises, or even by practice, trial and error, and feedback. Then I'll explain why everything anyone needs to know about writing can and must be learned by reading.

Hazards of Instruction

Formal writing instruction usually begins with the copying of letters and a few words, some rudimentary punctuation, minimal grammar, and a good deal of spelling (which is usually phonics in reverse). Most of this instruction is wasted, and much of it causes confusion and mutual frustration. Probably more potential writers are lost at this period of their education than at any other time.

Why are these "mechanics" emphasized at the beginning of writing education? I suspect simply because they are more manageable, more easily delivered as isolated units of instruction, and more easily marked and counted for record-keeping purposes. It may all appear obvious to anyone familiar with writing, but to a beginner, trying to make sense of written language, it can all be nonsense.

Consider *punctuation.* There is no punctuation in spoken language. We may pause at any time in speech for breath or rumination, but usually not at the spot where commas or periods are placed in writing. Instead there is a compulsion to talk of abstract *rules* which only make sense to someone who can already write. Consider one of the most basic rules: that a sentence begins with a capital letter and ends with a period. But we never tell learners what a sentence is—except by the circularity that it is something that begins with a capital letter and ends with a period. To say a sentence is a complete thought is meaningless— how can anyone explain what a complete thought is? And can't some sentences contain just half a thought, or a couple of thoughts? Certainly. (How many thoughts were contained in that last one-word sentence?)

Consider *spelling.* Phonics is practically useless—think of all the rules and exceptions I discussed in Chapter 3. Peepul hoo rite fonetikly are terrible spellers. The only way to learn to spell is to remember spellings. (A few simple rules may help as reminders when you are already a writer and speller.) But this doesn't mean spelling lists. The memorization of lists is the worst way to learn anything. Infants don't learn to talk by memorizing lists of words; they effortlessly learn new words when they hear them meaningfully used in everyday conversation. Most literate people know many thousands of spellings, but only a few hundred at best could come from lists of spellings or by attention to isolated words. Spellings are learned in the course of reading, in the manner I shall describe.

Very little is learned by talking or reading about *grammar,* either in spoken or written language. No one tells infants about nouns, verbs, and adjectives, let alone agreement, and vast numbers of people become articulate speakers and readers without ever learning the meaning of those labels. As I have just pointed out, discussion of sentences, phrases, and even words (as units of language) is meaningless unless the learner is already a writer. Paragraphing is a matter of style, not rules.

Feedback, through the correction of errors in exercises or in materials written by learners, can have a devastating effect on children at the threshold of the club of writers. Highlighting their "errors" doesn't help them become better writers; it only teaches them what they *can't* do. Children whose spelling mistakes are consistently marked usually learn that these are words they can't spell, and avoid them in the future (even if correct spellings are thoughtfully provided). The more children's writing is corrected, the less they tend to write. Simply given a score or a letter grade for any aspect of writing doesn't do a thing for the ability of learners, though it does for their self-image.

So have I made learning to write sound hopeless? I've just tried to explain what can make such formal instruction overwhelmingly difficult. Now I can discuss how learning to write can become far less stressful and much more productive and satisfying. It's all done through reading.

The Advantages of Reading

What is the value of reading for writers?

To begin with, everything an aspiring writer needs to know is available in print—not as precepts, but as practice. A book demonstrates how every word in that book is spelled, how every sentence is punctuated, and how every paragraph is organized. The more books a learner reads, the more demonstrations are provided. Extensive reading is essential for learning both to read and to write, which is why it is a tragedy that rich and interesting reading materials are often not made available to learners, and may even be taken away as libraries close, all in the name of educational efficiency.

The particular advantage of reading for aspiring writers is that learning itself is taken care of; there is no need for effort, practice, and disappointment. Someone else takes care of the learning, just as in learning to talk. With talking, someone else says, "Pass the ketchup please" or "Let's watch a movie this evening," and what is said becomes part of what the child can say. There is no need for practice, correction, failure, or even awareness. Adults (or friends) say something, and children have learned to say it themselves. The learning is not even imitation or modeling, but *vicarious.* One person does something, and as a consequence someone else instantly learns. It is the same for adults, of course. The only requirement for learning, for talkers or writers, is that you have to see yourself as the kind of person who does that kind of thing; you have to be a member of the club. It is the matter of identity again.

Of course, many of us read and don't learn a thing about writing. That inevitably occurs if we don't see ourselves as writers. Children who have become convinced that learning to write is not for them, who see themselves as *not* being writers, automatically exclude themselves from the club.

If you see yourself as a writer, you *read like a writer,* which means that you read as if you might be writing what you are at the moment reading. It's a vicarious activity resulting in vicarious learning. You read, and you learn something about writing like the author who wrote what you are reading. In a way, the reader is writing along with the author.

This is not a specialized talent. Children do not need to be taught to see themselves as members of the club of readers or of the club of writers. Their natural tendency is to see themselves as capable of doing anything—until experience or instruction teaches that idea out of them. Professional writers know that if you aspire to write like a particular author, you read what that author has written. You don't *study* how the author writes, you *participate* in the author's writing.

There's ample evidence that children are sensitive to what they read, even if they—and their teachers—are not aware of the fact. It doesn't always work in the learner's interest. Children whose reading primers were mindless three-line "stories"—*Spot is a dog. He wags his tail. He is happy.*—wrote similarly mindless fragments themselves when asked to compose a story. Children who were reading rich, complex, meaningful material produced stories that were creative and interesting. As computer programmers say: *garbage in, garbage out.*

As children become readers they can identify with the *characters* they read about, as exemplified in the books of many best-selling children's authors. When you are a member of the club of readers, you can become a member of any club in the world. But learners can also identify with the *authors* whose material they read, and then they can acquire another invaluable club membership. They can become members of the club of writers, with access to all the special knowledge, privileges, and assistance that more experienced members of that club can provide.

You learn to write by reading, but this is not to say that writing is not important. Writing helps learners to see themselves as writers. They identify with authors. "Correction" now can be invaluable, if it is provided in the form of suggestion and editing to *help* produce a piece of written work, rather than to highlight errors. But now it should be the learner who demands the essential feedback, not in order to know where mistakes have been made, *but in order to do it better.* The teacher becomes a collaborator. Ideally, the learner will be offended if mistakes are not indicated, but only because members of the club of writers naturally want to make what they create as professional as possible.

THE ELECTRONIC CLUB OF READERS

If reading is defined as "making sense of written language," then reading is no different in our electronic age than it has been in the past. The eyes and brain of today's readers are already primed for anything that present and future reading situations may present. What is different is the range of situations in which there are opportunities for reading, and new aspects of written language to be made sense of.

Reading has never been a simple matter of making sense of print on paper. Written language is already encountered in a variety of media—not just on paper, but on wood, stone, metal, plastic, internal and external walls, billboards, clothing, appliances, small and large screens, and even the sky itself. Written language is manifested not just in ink, but in carvings, inscriptions, light, smoke, flashing dots, negative spaces, and cunningly contrived assortments of anything from potted plants to crowds at sporting events.

Letters and words are frequently amorphous and unstable, changing in every attribute, wandering in all directions, and flashing on and off. They may be accompanied by contrapuntal images, illustrations, graphics, sound effects, voices, music, and other forms of distraction. The ability of the human brain to create order out of chaos is truly remarkable. Consider the complexity of reading material on "educational" television programs for children and in commercial announcements for everyone, where individual letters and words mutate in size, shape, color, and position like manic protoplasmic organisms. Reading is already a complex business—but people can be adaptable, especially young people.

The most effective way to become a reader on the Internet is the same as becoming a reader in any medium—voluntary membership in the club, with experience rather than specific instruction and with the author of the text being read still the most potent guide. The Internet may be a great place to get reading experience, but unhappily it is also a powerful medium for delivering specific instruction.

THE LITERACY CLUB ON-LINE

There is no reason why children (and adults) should have difficulty learning to read in the world of the Internet. Books may still (for the moment) be of greater utility and convenience to most children and most parents because books are familiar, convenient, portable, and (relative to computers) disposable. You can do all kinds of things with a book that you can't do with a monitor, like turn pages rapidly, make notes in the margin, share it with a friend, and take it to bed with you. On the other hand, you can do all kinds of things with a computer that you can't do with a printed book, like insert your own drawings and words in the text, change the appearance of the type, and print your own personal copies of pages.

Children can be just as intrigued by a story on a monitor as by one on book pages, and also by the electronic illustrations, which can be animated and accompanied by sound effects. And it's almost as easy to seat a child on your lap in front of a computer as with a book. Children can manipulate keys as easily as pages, they can read incoming e-mails as easily as letters coming in envelopes, and they can have the added excitement of receiving instant responses to their own writing.

The learner's interest is still critical, and the author remains the person who will actually teach reading (and writing), on-line or not. The same principles of club membership apply on-line—other people show you what can be done with language (and with the technology) and help you do these things yourself.

Computers can also stimulate reading on their own account. Learners frequently find a need to consult the manuals for the devices they use (especially if the manuals happen to be comprehensible), and learners can be inspired to read books about computers and the kinds of things computers can do. Many electronic games come with complex written instructions. For children, computers can be interesting things to work on and to think, talk, read, and write about, even when the children's particular interests are as diverse as art, music, science, or sports.

But as many teachers know, it may be as a tool for writing that computers can most help literacy. Word processors combine ease and speed with the flexibility of pencil and paper. There is no easier way to get ideas into written language—to erase, revise, move things around, edit, store, and recover. Few professional writers reject word processors once they get to know them, even though they may have used (or refused to use) electric typewriters for years. Anything that makes the act of writing easier makes learning to write easier.

There are other advantages of word processors not so widely appreciated or welcomed, for example, in checking spelling and suggesting vocabulary. There is no longer need to worry about the spelling of those awkward words that always defeat us, or to interrupt the flow of thought while we consult a dictionary. Just put down anything, even an initial letter, and the computer will sort it all out against its own spelling list when the composition is done. There is no need to go to the thesaurus for the word so irritatingly on the tip of your tongue. A touch of the key can provide a set of synonyms (or antonyms) for any notion we have in mind. There are grammar checkers, outline organizers, and the beginnings of systems that scrutinize for style and sense.

Some teachers object to these time-saving and labor-saving facilities for the same reason that there have been doubts about the use of calculators in classrooms—that they may make attention to basic skills unnecessary and therefore interfere with learning. But it's a mistake to believe that obstacles are the most efficacious motivators; there is no evidence that making an activity difficult facilitates learning. Quite the reverse. Lack of knowledge of spelling and vocabulary reduces the amount of writing that is done, especially when mistakes are penalized. A comfortable facility with reading and writing, on the other hand, makes learning the "basics" both continual and effortless.

Computers can take care of two of the greatest concerns of beginning and fluent writers alike: legibility and speed. Legibility is always a problem for writers, especially inexperienced young ones, even if not at the fetish level that neatness occasionally reaches in classrooms. One touch of a computer key and anyone has a perfectly formed letter that can be printed in a compact and properly aligned orientation. And precisely the same letter form can be replicated at will. No need even to remember that in English print goes from left to right, from top to bottom.

Computers help everyone write. And what helps writing helps and promotes reading. I haven't just been talking about the composition of books or of complicated documents and school assignments. I have in mind all the literacy club activities that can provide the opportunities for learning—correspondence, labels, lists, notes, memoranda, newspapers, magazines, reviews, digests, advertisements, plans, schedules, recipes, and timetables, with every thread of the fabric of living language, in actual or in virtual locations.

New kinds of reading materials are developing. With *hypertext*, which is text with no beginning, middle, or end, you can start reading at any point, jump to new topics whenever you wish, and stop whenever you feel inclined. There is no "right way" of reading the material; no two people may ever read it in the same way. But "nonlinear" organizations of text aren't new. Printed encyclopedias, dictionaries, and directories have always been organized on a nonnarrative basis—you read one item, and your interest may take you to new topics elsewhere in the book, behind as well as in front of where you are at present, and then on to others. There's nothing different about behaving in this way electronically, except that the range of choices is always very much greater (including narratives as well as other kinds of text) and the facility with which you can move to new areas is very much easier. As a result, you are always likely to encounter something that you haven't sought or anticipated, and possibly don't want. Experienced readers have always *browsed* and *scanned*; now there is *surfing*, akin to estimation in calculation, getting an approximate sense without laborious attention to detail.

New forms of writing are always arising, not only in new text formats but in novel conventions of spelling or abbreviating words, of phrasing questions and responses, of salutations and expressions of mood ;-). These are not arbitrary or ignorant forms of established language practices, they are new conventions that have developed to suit a new medium. Expected ways of relating to other people establish themselves in electronic interactions just as they do in other social settings. And what is new and required of writers can be easily learned by readers—if they read like writers.

The Wave of Technology

Educational institutions, from kindergarten to university, are relying more and more on technology to educate—and to teach reading. This is a different matter, concerned less with learning than with teaching. Learning will never change, but teaching will, and this comes down to an important issue in electronic education, the question of "Who's in charge?"

For this we must turn to the matter of teaching.

SUMMARY

To learn to read, children must see ways of employing reading to further their own aims and interests. If written language is made meaningful to them, they will learn in exactly the same way that they learn about spoken language. Children need others to read to them, and for them, until they can read for themselves. Children must be fully accepted into the club of readers so that they can receive all the different kinds of demonstration and collaboration they require to become readers themselves. By joining the club of writers, readers can learn to become writers, too.

CHAPTER 10

The Importance of Teachers

Blind faith in prepackaged methods or materials won't help more children become literate, no matter how much the methods and materials are officially sponsored, mandated, and monitored through tests. The reason is simply stated: *Children can't be taught to read.* But they can certainly be helped to learn. A teacher's responsibility is not to instruct children in reading but to make it possible for them to learn to read. There is a difference.

I have demonstrated that the real skills of reading, which have made readers out of you and me, aren't skills that are formally taught at school or ever could be. I am referring to such matters as the economical use of visual information and versatile memory management, reading for meaning rather than word by word. We have acquired these skills only through the practice of reading. Most of the time we aren't even aware of what these skills are and when and how we acquired them. And they certainly aren't matters explained to a majority of teachers or parents, or even, for that matter, to those who might benefit most from learning that reading is accomplished through experience rather than instruction—the individuals who are learning to read.

I have also shown that children "know" implicitly how to solve the problems of learning to read. And indeed, children must be trusted to know how to learn at a time that is appropriate for them, though not necessarily convenient for the school. What, then, is the role of the teacher? What is the point of "teaching reading" in school?

What takes place in the classroom is critical for many children, because it can determine whether they become readers or not. By consolidating membership in the club of readers, a teacher can be one of the most important people in the beginning reader's life. Schools may not be held wholly responsible for the degree to which children succeed in becoming literate. Nevertheless, teachers have a crucial part to play.

HELPING, NOT HINDERING

Children who come to school already members of the literacy club, who regard themselves as the kind of people who read and write, should find expanded opportunities in school for engaging in all the activities of club membership. Children who haven't become members before they arrive in school should find the classroom the place where they are immediately welcomed into the club. The classroom should be a place for meaningful and useful reading (and writing) activities, where participation is possible without coercion or evaluation and where collaboration is always available. No child should be excluded.

Children have to make sense of reading; therefore teachers must ensure that reading—and learning to read—makes sense to children. Children learn to read by reading; therefore teachers must help children read by making reading easy, not by making it difficult. These remarks may sound obvious, except for the fact that a good deal that is done at school—and also by well-meaning adults out of school—may have the consequence of making learning to read less comprehensible and more difficult. Because a major concern of a teacher must always be to avoid getting in the way of children's learning to read, I shall begin my specific remarks about the role of teachers with a list of negatives. I call the items on this list "easy ways to make learning to read difficult," because all too often they are urged upon teachers as rules that are supposed to help children to read. Later I become far more positive.

NINE FALLACIES OF READING INSTRUCTION

There are nine fallacies of reading instruction that teachers and parents would do well *not* to follow.

Fallacy 1. Aim for Early Mastery of the Rules of Reading

There are no rules of reading, at least none that can be specified with sufficient precision to make a child a reader. The implicit knowledge of how to read that experienced readers have acquired has been developed through reading, not through exercises or drills. Only reading provides the necessary practice in

- Identifying meaningful words on sight (not by figuring them out letter by letter)
- Using prior knowledge and context to identify words and meanings with a minimum of visual information (not struggling blindly and pointlessly to identify one word after another)
- Predicting, looking for meaning, reading quickly rather than slowly and confidently rather than cautiously
- Using short-term memory efficiently so that it's not overloaded, which can make even the most meaningful of texts into nonsense

Most of the drills that are supposed to help children read become useful—and easy—only after skill in reading has been developed. Better readers are always more efficient at knowing the alphabet, reciting the "sounds of letters," and "blending letter sounds together to make words," because these extraneous tasks become simple with experience in reading. But they are difficult if not impossible before children become readers.

Fallacy 2. Ensure that Phonic Rules Are Learned and Used

Children don't need a mastery of phonics in order to identify words that they haven't met in print before. The very complexity and unreliability of the 166 rules and scores of exceptions make it remarkable that anyone should think that inability to use phonics explains "why Johnny still can't read." Once a child discovers what a word is in a meaningful context, learning to recognize it on another occasion is as simple as learning to recognize a face on a second occasion and doesn't need phonics. Discovering what a word is in the first place is usually most efficiently accomplished by using context to provide a substantial clue, hearing someone else read the word, or asking someone.

Fallacy 3. Teach Letters or Words One at a Time, Making Sure Each One Is Learned Before Moving On

Another widespread misconception is that children have difficulty remembering the names of objects and words and letters, and that only constant repetition will help fix a name in a child's mind. Children from about the age of 2 learn at least 1,000 new words a year, often after hearing a word used only once or twice. It has been calculated that 8-year-old children learn nearly 30 new words daily. Children don't get credit for such remarkable feats of learning because the learning takes place so effortlessly and inconspicuously.

Few of these words are learned by rote—by children memorizing lists of a dozen new words at a time or by doing exercises given to them by adults. By criticizing phonics I'm not recommending a "whole-word" approach, or the mindless use of flashcards. Children learn by making sense of words that are meaningful to them in context; they learn through comprehension. We haven't become fluent readers by learning how to recognize 50,000 or more written words on sight; we have learned to recognize all these words in the process of becoming fluent readers, in the act of meaningful reading.

Fallacy 4. Make Word-Perfect Reading a Prime Objective

Because of the limit on the amount of incoming visual information from the eyes that the brain can handle, and the limit on how much can be retained in short-term memory, emphasis on visual information makes reading difficult. To read efficiently—and also to learn to read—it's necessary to make maximum use of what is already known. It usually doesn't matter if readers fail to get a word or two exactly right—provided they are looking for sense—because context will make it clear if an error that makes a difference has been made. On the other hand, concern with accuracy directs too much attention to individual words, in effect treating them as if they had no context, with the result that the visual system is overwhelmed. Most children seem to know intuitively that reading is a matter of getting meaning correct rather than identifying particular words, no doubt because the strain of focusing attention on words in isolation makes reading a difficult and nonsensical activity.

Fallacy 5. Discourage "Guessing"; Insist that Children Read Carefully

I have stressed the importance of prediction in comprehension and in the identification of unfamiliar words. Efficient readers make maximum use of a minimum of visual information because taking too many pains to avoid making mistakes will have the paradoxical effect of impeding comprehension and accuracy.

Even in learning to read—in fact, especially in learning to read—slowness has only one consequence: It adds to the burden on short-term memory, making comprehension less likely and thus making reading more difficult. For children, as for fluent readers, the only practical solution at times of difficulty is to speed up, to read on, and to try to find the general sense that will make it possible to go back, if necessary, to identify or comprehend specific words.

Reading has been described as a "guessing game," but I try to avoid that expression. The word *guessing* has negative connotations for many teachers and parents. It is associated with reckless or desperate behavior—or with attempts to achieve something without proper effort. *Prediction*—the elimination of unlikely alternatives—is a better word because it refers to a skilled activity, the use of prior knowledge to anticipate the future. Prediction is the basis of reading and of learning to read; it is the natural foundation of all meaningful activities.

Fallacy 6. Insist Upon Accuracy All the Time

No one can learn names correctly, whether of dogs and cats, letters or words, unless there is a possibility of being wrong. The "experimental" hypothesis-testing basis of learning necessitates taking chances. Children learn naturally, not by rote memorization or by reckless guessing but by trying to assess whether something might be the case. Adults who regard reading errors as stupidities, jokes, or transgressions—and who encourage children to do the same—do more than misperceive the basic nature of reading. They block a principal way in which reading is learned.

Many of the apparent mistakes that children make in reading aloud are not errors of sense. Rather, they reflect inability to do an additional task at the same time as reading for sense, namely, speaking in a language that is unfamiliar. It's not uncommon for any reader—beginner or experienced—to read aloud a sentence like *Back she came* as "She came back," or *He has no money* as "He hasn't any money" or even "He ain't got no money." The reader is getting the meaning of the text and is putting it into a familiar language, the way the reader would normally talk. It's unreasonable to expect children not only to understand text but to speak aloud in a particular language register that may seem forced, artificial, and even nonsensical to them.

Fallacy 7. Correct Errors Immediately

A guaranteed way to make children anxious, hesitant, and otherwise inefficient readers is to pounce on errors the moment they occur. This discouraging habit is sometimes justified as "providing immediate feedback," but, in fact, it may not be relevant to what the child is trying to do, and may in the long run discourage children from relying on their own judgment for self-correction when they have made a mistake.

Not only can correction and other "assistance" come too soon, it can also be misguided. A child reading aloud who pauses before a word is frequently supplied with that word instantly, by other children if not by the teacher. But the pause may not reflect doubt about that particular word. The child may already have made a tentative silent identification and be wondering what that word has to do with words that have already been read or even with what the child can see coming up a few words ahead. Once again, a word-by-word emphasis can have the result of persuading a learner that reading is an activity in which sense plays little part.

Fallacy 8. Identify and Treat Problem Readers as Early as Possible

There are many reasons why children may seem to make slow progress at the beginning of learning to read. They may not yet understand what reading is about, they may not be interested in reading, they may be apprehensive about the teacher or other adults who want them to learn to read, or they may resent the whole idea of school. They may not understand the language in which their schoolbooks are written or the language that their teacher uses to talk about reading. They may even have started off on the wrong foot, for example, by assimilating the notion that if they learn how to decode and identify individual words, then sense will take care of itself.

There are two reasons why identifying such children as "problem readers"—or as challenged, at-risk, or learning-disabled in some way—is not a good way to help them. The first reason is that children so labeled immediately become anxious and don't expect to perform as well as other children. Their general perception of their own abilities suffers, and they exclude themselves from the club of readers. Such attitudes are completely disabling, even for competent readers. They may begin to strive excessively to avoid mistakes, pay far too much attention to every word, and become practically blinded by tunnel vision and the overload on short-term memory. To label children as "problem readers" early in their lives may create a problem where there was none originally.

The second reason why the label of "poor reader" can be so disabling to learners—all the way through their school careers—is that teachers and others immediately start treating the learner differently. Very often the "solution" for such a condition is more of the same treatment that caused the confusion in the first place. The victims find themselves excluded from the club of readers even if they want to belong. Children identified as "poor readers" are often deprived of opportunities to read and given the much harder task of trying to sound out isolated words or words in meaningless sequences. Students who have had reading problems for years don't need more of the treatments that have contributed to their condition.

Fallacy 9. Use Every Opportunity During Reading Instruction to Improve Spelling and Written Expression, and Also Insist On the Best Possible Spoken English

Being able to spell has nothing to do with reading ability. We can all read words that we can't spell, and being able to spell a word does little to help us read it. I'm not saying that spelling and other language skills aren't important, but that they can complicate a reading task. If the aim at one particular time is to help a child become fluent in reading, expecting the child also to worry about answering questions, writing answers, and avoiding errors of spelling or grammar is simply to overload the reading task and to make learning to read more difficult.

Similarly, spoken English is largely irrelevant to reading. Children forced to worry about their pronunciation as they read aloud won't become better readers (nor will their speech be improved). Expecting children to read in what to them may be a completely unnatural style may give a totally false idea of what reading is.

HELPING CHILDREN LEARN TO READ

Two questions perhaps arise. The first is that it's all very well for me to provide a set of negative statements about what teachers should endeavor to avoid; what should a teacher do? If there is little sense in a lot of drill and exercise, what instead should be going on in the reading classroom? The second question is that my list of cautions about hampering children who are learning to read implies that the children are already capable of some reading in the first place. What does a teacher do about a child who can't read at all? How does a teacher get children started in the club of readers? The answers to both questions are the same, because there is basically only one problem: how to facilitate reading for children when they can read very little or not at all. The answers can be summed up in one basic rule and guideline for every aspect of reading instruction—*make learning to read easy*—which simply means making reading a meaningful, enjoyable, useful, and frequent experience for children.

Put in another way, the solution requires that teachers ensure that written material is available that every individual child will find of interest and that someone, who could be another child, is at hand to help read this interesting material when children can't read it for themselves. If a child can't read at all, the teacher or other helpful reader must do all the reading for the child.

Reading to and with children helps them to achieve three important objectives in beginning to read and continuing to learn to read:

1. *Understanding the functions of print.* It is in being read to, or read with, that children find the opportunity to gain the insight that print has purposes. Children can't be *told* that written language is a varied part of the environment that can be as meaningful, useful, and satisfying as speech. Children must *experience* that insight for themselves; they must be put into situations in which the insight can develop.

2. *Gaining familiarity with written language.* Spoken and written language are put together in distinctive ways. The particular conventions of written language can make it quite unpredictable, and therefore difficult to comprehend, for anyone not familiar with them. Constructions that are common in children's books,

such as *What splendid teeth the beaver has* or *Down the road hand in hand ran Susie and her friend*, seem simple and straightforward to most of us only because of our familiarity with written language, but they aren't the kind of language anyone is likely to encounter in everyday speech. The only way children can become familiar with written language, before they can extend their knowledge by reading for themselves, is by being read to.

3. *Getting the chance to learn.* It is important to read *to* children, but even more important to read *with* them. Children get their first chance to solve many of the problems of reading when they and adults are reading the same text at the same time. It doesn't matter that at the beginning the children may recognize none of the words they are looking at; indeed, it's in the process of being confronted by words that are unknown that they find the motivation and opportunity to begin naturally to distinguish and recognize particular words. Children reading along with an adult or other reader will look out for the words that they know, and they will select for themselves the additional words that they want to learn.

An interesting change takes place as an adult and child read together. Initially, the child's eyes wander all over the pages (or focus on the pictures), but soon the eyes begin to follow along behind the words as the child strives to grasp some understanding of the relationship between the marks on the page and what is being said—the adult is reading *to* the child. But as the child develops a little proficiency in reading, especially if the passage being read is from a poem or story well known to the child, then the child's eyes move ahead of the reader's voice. The child begins reading independently of the adult assistance, and the adult is reading *with* the child. The situation is not unlike learning to ride a bicycle. For as long as the child needs adult help, then the child cycles slower than the adult pushes. But as competence and confidence develop, the child tends to pull ahead of the adult until eventually able to manage alone. The child no longer needs the adult.

There is no need to fear that a child who is helped at the beginning will become lazy or overly dependent on adults. The child able to take over from the adult in reading will be no more content to lag behind than the child riding the bicycle. Mastery provides its own incentives.

Children who can tie their own shoelaces rarely tolerate adults who insist on doing it for them.

MAKING SENSE OF ALL KINDS OF PRINT

In stressing the importance of reading to children, I don't want to give the impression that I'm talking just about books. In fact, I think that the widespread emphasis on books in school can often be obstructive. Indeed, the only books that should be read to children or that they should be required to read for themselves are the ones that genuinely interest them, that contain fascinating rhymes and stories rather than the bland and unnatural prose to which many children are expected to attend, whether recounting a boring day in the life of an insipid pair of fictitious children or relating that *Sam can fan Dan.*

The print that offers beginning readers the most insights into the meaningfulness of written language tends to lie outside books in the far more personal and pervasive world of their own lives. Children may learn more of the basics of reading from the brand name above a gas station, the words on a candy wrapper, or the experience of their own name beside a coat hook, than from any number of books and exercises. In natural, out-of-school surroundings, printed words don't exist to be associated with sounds, but with sense. Chalked on a board in the classroom or printed below a picture in a book, the letters T-O-Y-S have no function, no point. But when the same marks occur in a store or on the lid of a storage box, they convey the distinct and important meaning, "This is where the toys can be found."

The wealth of meaningful print in the environment of children can be read to them, not in any obtrusive or demanding manner but as casually and naturally as the objects in a child's environment are named. Just as children are told "There's a big dog" or "See the plane up there?" so adults can say "That says *ketchup*" and "There's the *one-way* sign." This simple practice will give children the opportunity to derive insights, generate ideas, and test hypotheses about reading while they retain the freedom to select and control what they are most likely to learn whenever it makes the most sense to them. In such circumstances children learn about print and about reading in the same way that they learn about spoken language, without obvious effort or the need for formal instruction.

READING IN SCHOOL

Total immersion in meaningful print is hardly a typical experience for many children in school, nor indeed can all the conditions that facilitate learning to read be easily translated into the classroom. It is difficult for teachers to duplicate the richness of print that occurs naturally in the outside world, an example of the many differences between school and the world at large that children can find so confusing.

Nevertheless, there are many ways in which children in school can experience printed language that has both interest and meaning for them. Teachers can try to ensure that children often have the opportunity to read—or to hear—stories that have an intrinsic appeal, to which they will voluntarily give attention. Teachers can also make frequent use of print to forward a significant activity in some way, whether in play (keeping a store, publishing a newspaper) or in the daily routine.

Printed materials and products that make sense to children in the outside world can be brought into the classroom. And there are a number of ways in which print can be emphasized in the functions of the school, for example, in the identification of various classrooms and offices, restrooms and storage rooms, lockers and coat hooks (all of which are often labeled too high for young children's eyes). Menus—both the restaurant and the computer variety—constitute meaningful print, and so do posters, notices, direction signs, maps, catalogs, timetables, and telephone books, especially if they can be produced in a format children can handle, a print they can discriminate easily, and a language they can understand. Not only can these and other familiar materials be used to help children learn more about reading, but they also offer the only opportunity many children may have of learning to use or make sense of the materials themselves. And, of course, much of it can be produced by the children. No one ever learned to use a telephone directory from a lecture; experience at a specific task, with friendly help in meaningful situations, makes the learning of any skill possible.

At the same time that an abundance of meaningful print is provided, much of the print that is meaningless could be removed from the scene. There may be occasional justification for the use of individual letters and even isolated words as part of the decor, and lists of useful words (like the days of the week or months of the year) can at times have value for reference purposes. But, in general, the tendency should be resisted to decorate walls with sheets of print whose only function is to give the impression of an educational atmosphere, for adults as well as for children. There is usually little need for a frenzy of alphabetic decoration at the expense of windows, pictures, and even soothing sections of blank wall.

Of course, providing a print-rich environment and endeavoring to avoid interference with the natural ability of children to learn doesn't constitute a "program" or "system" for reading instruction. I can't provide a consumers' report on all the different reading methodologies. The only conclusion to draw from the analysis I have made is that no one can rely on a package on a shelf or ordered from a publisher to teach reading. Reading isn't taught by prescription. There are hundreds of reading programs, many of which have little relevance to reading. And even the most sensible of programs will be little more than an aid to keeping children occupied while they are learning to read.

Reading can't be taught in the way that arithmetic is often taught (not always successfully, either), as a sequence of units that can be ticked off and taken for granted as children show proficiency in each one. "Systematic instruction" scarcely scratches the surface of reading.

Teachers must make their own decisions about what needs to be done in the classroom. The question shouldn't be "Which method should I use?" but "How do I decide what to do now?" I haven't argued that there should be no phonics, only that phonics has a widely unsuspected complexity and that children should be expected to learn about phonics only to the extent that they can make sense of the instruction, after they have joined the club of readers. I haven't said that children should not learn the alphabet (it helps teachers and children communicate on the subject of written language), but until children have a good idea of what reading is, reciting the names of letters is largely a nonsensical activity. The concern should always be with what a child can make sense of, something that can't be anticipated by anyone who doesn't know the child. Distant "experts" should not be expected to make decisions for teachers.

I'm certainly not arguing that teachers shouldn't know about the tools of their trade, about the multitude of programs, materials, and activities that are available for their use. The training teachers receive on the subject of reading may be totally devoted to lectures and demonstrations about different programs and methods. Frequently lacking is any kind of discussion of the nature of reading, so that teachers can make up their own minds about when and how to use particular methods for the particular children in their classrooms. Teachers often don't know what programs can reasonably be expected to accomplish—how much, for example, a child can actually learn from phonic and phonemic awareness drills, or from sound-blending exercises—nor do they know the cost of such programs to the child in terms of memory overload, tunnel vision, rote learning, boredom, or confusion. The classroom task often becomes teaching the activity that is prescribed by the program or curriculum, not responding to the learner's need or the teacher's intentions. Teachers must be discriminating, and that requires both a familiarity with programs and an understanding of reading. They must be able to see what makes sense.

Where teachers can't save children from engaging in pointless activities and undergoing ritualistic tests, they can at least explain to children the difference. Children can understand that they might be asked to do something just to keep them quiet, or because some authority arbitrarily wants it. The tragedy is when children are led to believe that the boring or threatening activities *are* reading.

Many children have learned to read without special programs or materials at all, and many other children have learned despite their formal instruction. Everything I have said about reading in this book is contrary to approaches that demand sequenced instruction and constant measurement and is therefore contrary to instruction teachers may themselves receive in their own training.

PROBLEMS OF PROGRAMMATIC INSTRUCTION

I have been critical of programs a number of times in this book and even more forcefully elsewhere. It's time perhaps for me to explain exactly what I am referring to by the term *programs*, why they tend to be misguided if not totally wrong, and why nevertheless they are so pervasive in education and might become even more so.

By *programs*, or *programmatic instruction*, I refer to any endeavor by anyone outside the classroom to determine systematically and in advance what teachers and learners should do next in the classroom. Programmatic instruction typically involves predetermined activities, drills, exercises, prerequisites, questions and responses, right and wrong

answers, scores, marks, grades, tests (many tests), objectives, entry behaviors, target behaviors, criterion levels, and "accountability." Such
instruction rarely engages children in meaningful reading enterprises
(except in the mind of the program developer). The written language
that is demonstrated, and to which children are expected to attend,
tends to be fragmented, decontextualized, and trivial. When "authentic
texts," or "real books," are used, they may be simplified, bowdlerized,
and debased with reams of pointless commentary and intrusive inter-
rogation. If anything, all of these aspects of programs teach that written
language is problematical or nonsensical and doesn't warrant serious
attention. Many program developers entertain the amazing belief that
reading can be taught to a child one predetermined bit at a time—on
computer monitors as well as on paper.

All of this is the antithesis of admitting children to the club of readers. None of the drills, exercises, and tests of formal programmatic instruction demonstrates that written language is meaningful or useful;
their only purposes are their own instructional ends. The only evident
reason for children to attend to the task is to get it over with, to get a
mark, or because the teacher says so.

Why, then, is so much reading instruction programmatic? Why do
school systems buy programs on a massive scale (which is the sole motivation for many publishers in this billion-dollar industry to produce
them)? One reason is that schools are strange institutions; one might
almost argue that they are designed to *prevent* the formation of clubs.
They are walled off from the meaningful world outside, with children
segregated into groups so homogenized in age and ability that they
are often unable to help each other, under the supervision of an isolated teacher with little time to engage personally in worthwhile literate
activities that the children can observe. Some teachers feel they need
programmatic activities just to keep the lid on, to escape chaos.

A second reason for the pervasiveness of programs in education is
inertia. Systematized instruction has been around for so long that many
people can't imagine education without it (just as many teachers can't
imagine learning taking place without constant tests and other forms of
evaluation, although these aren't characteristics of how children learn
spoken language and other things out of school). Schools of education
train new teachers to be dependent on programs, sometimes because
the professors know no better, sometimes because they can say it's what
schools want or because it's what schools are like.

A third reason for programmatic instruction is an egregious error in theory and practice—the belief that competence can be constructed one bit at a time in arbitrary sequences. Analyze in detail all the things an expert can do (so the belief goes), and then teach these things one at a time to a beginner, and the beginner will become an expert. Readers know the alphabet, so teach the alphabet. They can do phonics, so teach phonics. Readers seem to know what you are talking about when you refer to letters, words, and sentences, so teach definitions of letters, words, and sentences. All of this overlooks how or why experts acquired their skills in the first place and ends up getting most things backwards. Reading makes you good at the alphabet, phonics, and all the rest. Membership in the club of readers makes all the skills available to children. But insistence on separate skills as prerequisites for literacy simply keeps children out of the club.

Teachers need programs if they don't trust children to learn, if they fear that involvement in written language won't be sufficient to promote children's learning to read. And people outside the classroom insist on programs if they don't trust teachers to teach and feel they must be controlled every step of the way.

THE CHALLENGE OF TEACHING READING

The analysis of reading contained in this book can't immediately change the world for teachers. I don't expect that all teachers will find it easy or even feasible to put new insights that they have gained into practice. Teachers may feel they have few choices about what they actually do in the classroom and believe they are locked into a limited range of programs and procedures. They may work in unsuitable premises with too many children in competitive, anxious, and even hostile atmospheres. A frequent need to test, evaluate, and demonstrate "accountability" can induce tension and fear of failure in teacher and child alike.

Teachers may find it difficult to change their behavior for all kinds of reasons, including pressure from parents, the expectations of administrators, the resistance of colleagues threatened by any suggestion of disruption, the inertia of tradition in education, the dead weight of their own training, and the daily rituals and frustration in the classroom. The idea that learning should be made easy for children rather than "challenging" (a synonym for "making difficulties") can offend an ingrained puritanism—which infects children and parents—while a class in which everyone is happily reading something of personal interest may be criticized as a place where no "work" is being done.

Teachers can lack the time to think about fundamental change or the moral support they need in order to go through with it. Most children aren't angels—they don't settle down to learn what teachers would like them to learn in the cooperative way that may seem to have been implied in the discussions of this book or that is taken for granted by many formal programs. Children can be apathetic, aggressive, distracted, or obstinate for reasons that no amount of learning or understanding on the part of teachers can do very much about. All of these constitute problems for reading instruction, but they don't change the nature of reading or the way in which it must be learned.

Despite all the limitations on what teachers can do, they are still better off knowing more about what facilitates learning to read and what interferes with it. A new understanding won't directly change the world for teachers, but it can provide them with confidence to try to bring some changes about or simply to buck the trend. Understanding why certain conditions or activities make both learning and teaching more difficult can relieve the anxiety and minimize the consequences for teachers and children alike, particularly in terms of their self-respect.

Ultimately, teachers of reading may find they have to do most of their educating outside the classroom, teaching parents, administrators, and politicians the real way that children learn to read, and demonstrating that they, the teachers, know best how learners can be helped.

SUMMARY

Teachers must ensure that all children are admitted into the club of readers, where they can see written language employed in a variety of useful and meaningful ways and can receive assistance in employing written language themselves. Accuracy and "skills" should not be stressed at the expense of meaningfulness to the learner; they are a consequence rather than a prerequisite of reading experience. Teachers must protect themselves and their students from the effects of programs and tests, which can persuade learners that reading is nonsensical, painful, and pointless instead of satisfying, useful, and often joyful.

CHAPTER 11

Labels and Fables

It is evident that some children find learning to read harder than others, but there is little reason to believe that any children learn "differently"—that reading is a different kind of problem for them—and that therefore a different kind of instructional approach is required. The idea that some children are "verbal learners" and that others are "visual learners" is a myth. Except for the special cases of blind or severely hearing impaired individuals, all children learn both visually *and* verbally. Learning to talk and learning to read both recruit all available senses. Phonics doesn't work better for some children than for others. And when some major impairment intervenes, the solution for all learners is not to switch to some meaningless set of activities, but to be even more vigilant that the learner's experiences make sense.

A number of special issues frequently associated with reading instruction have not so far been discussed in this book. I'm referring to such topics as dyslexia, learning disability, remedial reading, readiness for reading, and dialect differences. None of these matters has anything directly to do with learning to read, but they certainly are relevant to reading instruction, because they can make a considerable difference to what a teacher does, or feels free to do, in the classroom. And, regrettably, these issues can make a considerable difference to the opportunities open to a child for learning to read. They are all labels and fables, indiscriminately applied and often devastating in their consequences.

DYSLEXIA

This term is a label, not an explanation or a medical condition. *Dyslexia* means, quite literally, being unable to read. Children who experience difficulty learning to read are frequently called dyslexic, but their difficulty doesn't arise because something in them makes them dyslexic, or because they have dyslexia; they are dyslexic because they can't read. To say that dyslexia is a cause of being unable to read is like saying that lameness is a cause of being unable to walk. We were all dyslexic at one stage of our lives and become dyslexic again whenever we are confronted by something that we can't read. The cure for dyslexia is to read.

It's a common belief, reflected in some dictionary definitions, that dyslexia is a medical condition resulting from a brain defect or malfunction. The origin of this belief is the incontrovertible medical fact that individuals once able to read may have their ability impaired as a consequence of damage to the brain from injury or illness, just as they may lose powers of speech or movement. Similarly, a child with a damaged brain may have difficulty learning to read. But such children will manifest other difficulties, too, and they constitute a very small proportion of all children indeed (very much smaller than the proportion of children who have difficulty learning to read). The fact that learning in general may be affected in rare cases of brain defect doesn't mean that a brain defect has caused a specific difficulty in learning to read. The latter view is so widespread that its rejection bears emphasis: *There is no convincing evidence that children who have difficulty learning to read but exhibit no other symptoms suffer from a brain defect or dysfunction.*

Obviously, children must be able to see and to understand language if they are to learn to read easily, but if these abilities are present there is no theoretical or medical reason why a child should fail to learn to read.

The notion that children can have a specific learning disability exclusive to reading as a consequence of brain malfunction is a fable. The term *specific learning disability* is, again, simply a label for an inadequately understood state of affairs, not an explanation. The learning disability is in fact deduced from the failure to read; the only evidence for the diagnosis is the very condition it is supposed to explain, rather like saying that fever is caused by having a high temperature. The lack of physical evidence for many reading difficulties is sometimes accounted for by the assertion that the brain defect or dysfunction is "minimal." In place of an acknowledgment that there might be no defect at all, the "explanation" is offered that the defect is so small as to be undetectable.

There are no specific learning disabilities in the sense that children who can see well enough to distinguish cars, animals, and people might not see well enough to read, or that children who understand language well enough to comprehend speech might still not be able to read. Obviously, children who can't see or comprehend speech well will have difficulty learning to read, but they have visual or language problems generally, not specific reading disabilities.

There are many reasons why children who cope perfectly well with the world and school in every other respect might show little progress in learning to read, ranging from anxiety or lack of interest to actually having the wrong idea of what reading is. Failure to learn to read doesn't require a medical diagnosis, and pseudomedical explanations for children whose only impairment seems to be in learning to read are not only unjustified, they are dangerous. Children regarded as brain-damaged are unlikely to be treated in the same way as children regarded as "normal." Teachers told that a child is dyslexic should always inquire into the symptoms of the disability; and if told that failure to read is the only symptom, they should understand that they are not being told anything they don't know already or couldn't find out without a specialist's diagnosis. If told that the dyslexia is a consequence of brain damage, they should ask how the handicap is manifested in other ways; and if told that the defect is minimal and restricted only to reading, they should recognize that the diagnosis is based on a poor understanding of reading and a complete lack of supporting evidence.

And, in any case, the only treatment for dyslexia, and any other kind of reading disability, real or imagined, is the same as the treatment for all learners: Help the child make sense of reading. The only difference is that more—often much more—time, patience, and understanding will probably be required.

REVERSALS

The tendency to give unnecessary and inaccurate medical explanations for quite normal kinds of behavior is well illustrated by the phenomenon of *reversals*—the apparent confusion of pairs of letters like *b* and *d* or *p* and *q*, and even pairs of words like *was* and *saw,* or *no* and *on*. Misreadings of this kind are conspicuous in some children and may provoke "treatment" that can make learning to read more difficult. In fact, the discrimination of mirror-image figures isn't easy, mistakes can be made by anyone, and the problem invariably goes away as the individual learns to read.

The discrimination of *b* from *d* is difficult because the difference between the two letters is minimal—a matter of whether the upright stroke is on the left or the right of the circle—and is not a difference that is significant or even relevant in most other aspects of our experience. A dog is a dog whether it is facing right or left; a car is a car whether it is traveling west or east. Only letters of the alphabet change their name depending on the direction they are facing. (Those more general discriminations that do require distinctions of actual or relative direction, such as "left" and "right" or telling time from the hands of a clock, are notoriously difficult for most children.)

Not only is the *b/d* distinction difficult for children learning to read because of its unusual and minimal nature, it's also one of the easiest for adults to confuse. Of course, we don't usually mistake *b* and *d* when we read, but that is primarily because we have so many other clues and aren't looking at the letters in the first place. Fluent readers could make sense of print if every *b* were changed into *d* and vice versa, or if every *b* and *d* were obliterated altogether. But to distinguish *b* from *d* when the letters occur in isolation, one at a time, is much harder, and the fact that we can normally do so with facility must be attributed to the years of experience we have had and the amount of time we are given, relatively speaking, to inspect the evidence. Put a fluent reader in a situation where a minimum of visual information is available—for example, by flashing the letter briefly on a screen—and there is a high probability that if a mistake is made at all it will be to confuse *b* with *d, p* with *q*.

Because the difference between *b* and *d* is both unusual and difficult to perceive, it's relatively difficult for children to learn, especially if they aren't given adequate opportunity to observe and practice making the distinction, or if they are confused about the distinction in the first place. Children can't "see" a difference if they don't understand what it is or the difference that it makes. It's a fable to assert that reversals are caused by "seeing backward." Seeing backward is a logical and physical impossibility. It's physically impossible to see part of our field of view one way and the rest the other—to see two cars going one way and one in the reverse direction when they are all in fact heading the same way. A child who sees a letter backward would have to see everything else backward at the same time, including the paper or board on which the letter was written. But it's logically impossible for everything to be seen backward, because each element would still be seen in the same relationship with every other element, and paradoxically therefore everything would still appear to be the right way around.

Sometimes it is argued that children must be seeing letters backward because they write them that way. But writing requires quite different kinds of skill altogether. We can all recognize faces and figures that we couldn't possibly reproduce accurately. If I try to draw a face and make it look like a potato, that doesn't mean that I see a face as a potato; it means that I'm a poor artist. A child may draw a human figure as a circular head with matchstick arms and legs, but the picture doesn't indicate how the child sees a human figure. Show young children their own distorted drawings of a person and an artist's representation, and they will readily tell you which looks more like what they see. Most children don't and can't draw what they see. The fact that they might write a few or many letters backward says nothing about their vision, but simply that they haven't yet learned the difficult task of writing letters conventionally.

How should a child who makes reversals be treated? Confronted by the choice of helping children to circumvent a minor difficulty or of magnifying it into a major stumbling block, teachers may unwittingly act as if they have no choice at all and select the most difficult and least productive alternative. The importance of being able to distinguish *b* from *d* is grossly overrated. Skill in making the distinction is not required to become a reader, but becoming a reader makes distinguishing the two letters relatively simple, especially when they occur in meaningful print. When children have trouble with letters, perhaps confusing words like *big* and *dig*, it must be because they are reading words or sentences that are essentially meaningless (or as if they are meaningless). No one who is reading for sense could confuse words like *big* and *dig*, or *was* and *saw*, in a meaningful context. No one reading for sense could read *I saw a big bird* as *I was a dig dird*.

But instead of being encouraged to use meaning to help unravel the confusion of similar-looking words, children who encounter difficulty are likely to be given concentrated exercises requiring them to distinguish word pairs like *big* and *dig* in isolation; this is not only more difficult but is almost certainly going to increase apprehension and bewilderment. And if they show no progress with words in isolation, the children may be restricted to drills with *b* and *d* alone. But letters in isolation are considerably more difficult than letters in words because an important clue has been removed. The difference between *b* and *d* at the beginning of a word is that the upright stroke is on the outside for *b* (as in *big*) but on the inside for *d* (as in *dig*). But "outside" and "inside" are meaningless terms for letters in isolation.

There is only one possible way of making learning to distinguish *b* and *d* even more difficult, and that is to show the letters one at a time, so that there is no basis for comparison, expecting children to learn *b* before even meeting *d*. This, of course, is the logical final step of transforming the "problem" of reversal from a transient nuisance to enduring impairment. The only treatment required to help a child avoid reversal errors is a solid regime of meaningful reading, so that a temporary difficulty is not magnified into an insurmountable handicap before the child learns to read.

READINESS

The question of when a child becomes ready to begin reading is frequently asked. But it is asked more as a matter of administrative convenience, concerned with whether reading instruction is likely to be productive, than to find out something meaningful about the child. Theoretically the question makes no sense at all. There is no miraculous day in a child's life, or degree of knowledge that a child must possess, when it can be said that the child passes from a state of being unable to learn to read to a state of being "ready." And there is certainly no test that will measure the state the child is in. There is no psychological or linguistic basis for the notion of "readiness"—it's a label and a fable. If learning to read is regarded as a continual process of making more and more sense of written language, advancing with every reading experience and beginning with the first insight that print is meaningful, then it will be seen that there can never be anything specific for a child to be ready for.

Children may at times lack interest in further reading, but it doesn't make sense to say that for some physical or intellectual reason they aren't ready to read more.

The term *readiness* as generally used in education doesn't really refer to readiness to read, nor even to readiness to learn to read, but to quite a different state of affairs, namely, readiness to cope with reading instruction. Everything depends on the way in which children are expected to learn. If the instruction emphasizes knowledge of the alphabet, then children who can't identify the letters won't be ready. If the instruction requires breaking down spoken words into imaginary sounds ("*cat* is kuh-a-tuh"), then children confused by this exercise won't be ready. Every instructional procedure demands its price of admission, and children who can't pay this price aren't ready to make sense of the instruction. They certainly won't benefit from it.

Reading and learning to read don't make exorbitant demands. Children need certain basic insights in order to develop as readers, but these insights come with reading (and with being read to), not with being deprived of reading experience. Reading demands visual acuity, but only the same acuity that a child uses in distinguishing familiar cars, animals, or faces. Reading demands language ability, but it is the same ability that is demonstrated in comprehending a familiar form of speech. Reading demands the ability to learn, but any child who has made sense of a familiar world outside school has that ability. There is no question of maturation here; none of this is a matter of waiting until a child is physically ready. As far as vision is concerned, the eyes reach their optimum efficiency at the age of 4. The same applies to auditory acuity, with the added qualification that it is not necessary to hear very well in order to read because reading doesn't involve decoding to sound. All that is desirable is to be able to hear what the teacher is talking about.

Inventories exist that claim to catalog all the prerequisites for readiness. They aren't usually informed by any kind of theory about the nature of reading but are more like "shopping lists" of everything the compiler thinks might be relevant to reading, ranging from "knowledge of letters and sounds" to physical and emotional maturity and even "correct body–book posture" (as if a child with no experience of reading should be expected to hold a book intelligently). But as I have already discussed, while it's true that children who know the alphabet, and who are good at phonics, and who understand terms like *word* and *sentence*, tend to be good readers, in each case the ability to read is a cause rather than a consequence of the particular skill. Obviously the child who is most ready to read is the child who can read already. (This is not such a facetious suggestion, because it's only children who can't read who are "not ready." Like the cure for dyslexia, readiness comes with reading.)

The reading problems that children experience reflect the instruction they are expected to make sense of. Only children in phonics classes have "poor auditory memories," while reversals are only found in classes where meaningless visual discriminations are involved. Similarly, the age at which reading problems occur reflects the age at which children are expected to learn to read. In countries where formal instruction starts at the age of 5, reading problems begin to appear among children aged 6. Where formal efforts to teach reading begin at age 8, reading problems don't arise until age 9. The child with the reading problem, or who isn't ready to read, is always the one who can't make sense of instruction at the time it is offered.

One might think that children have to be at just the right age and in the most favorable circumstances, if they are to learn to read. But the evidence is otherwise. Children need not be very "mature" to learn to read; many children of 3 and even 2 years of age have succeeded. But these children have other things to do than read, and few books are written that are of interest to 2-year-olds. Besides, it's not necessary to be very young to learn to read. Unlettered adults in the jungles of South America learn to read in less than 2 months once their instructors have found a way to engage their interest and have provided material that is relevant to them. It's not necessary to be very "privileged" materially to learn to read, or to speak with a particular dialect; many poor children in all cultures have succeeded in solving the problem. It's not even necessary to be very smart to learn to read; indeed, it's being able to read that makes many people seem so smart. And it's certainly not necessary to have specialized programs and materials to learn to read. The basic requirements are easily stated: an interest in learning to read (or, more precisely, in making sense of print) on the part of the learner, and, on the part of the teacher, the ability to find interesting print for the learner to make sense of. In the latter respect, teachers can be just as "unready" as learners.

Once again, I'm not saying that all children will learn to read effortlessly at any age; obviously that is not the case. Lack of interest, lack of confidence, and emotional problems will certainly be impediments, as will evident physical difficulties like poor vision or poor motor coordination. It is also always possible that something will go wrong with the instruction. But none of these are a matter of "readiness" in a physiological or intellectual sense.

Children shouldn't all be expected to learn to read at the same time or at the same rate or from the same materials, for the simple reason that children are individuals. This individuality may be an administrative inconvenience, but it is one that education must try to capitalize on rather than eradicate. Children who can't understand certain materials or activities from which they are expected to learn to read in school don't have a reading problem; the problem is the school's.

Children have reading problems when they read "below grade level." But grade levels have no reality outside the administrative organization of school; they certainly don't reflect any condition of the human brain. The fact that a 9-year-old reads like an average 8-year-old is not in itself cause for dismay. It doesn't mean that the child will never catch up. No one ever talks of a 30-year-old reading like a 29-year-old, and we all read like a beginner when we are having difficulty reading.

REMEDIAL READING

Children sometimes seem to come to a dead end in learning to read or to experience unusually severe difficulty in getting started. For such children, it's frequently argued that a different approach is required. It may be safe to leave children who are not having difficulty to direct and control their own learning, but for others a "more structured" program is called for. They are said to be "at risk"—although what they are at risk from, except the school system, is not revealed. They may be said to be in need of "recovery," though what they lost, and how they lost it, is not explained.

"Problem readers" are often said to need exercises and drills before exposure to meaningful reading. But the reverse is the case. Phonics is a cumbersome and unreliable system for any child, but especially for children finding it hard to make sense of reading. The analysis of spelling-to-sound correspondences that I have given in this book is a statement about the nature of language itself and can't be thought to hold true for some people but not for others. And it would be perverse to argue that a strategy of reading that won't work for good readers should be especially appropriate for children who find difficulty with reading.

Children who find it hard to make sense of reading need more meaningful reading, not less. Drilling children in a few simple letter-sound correspondences may seem to help them make progress in learning, but this progress should always be weighed against the degree to which it may persuade children that reading is not a meaningful activity. Paradoxically, children who don't learn to read easily are often expected to learn in the most difficult way possible. They may be assigned to remedial reading programs that are neither remedial nor reading. The most effective means of helping children of all ages who are in difficulty is to show them that reading is not a painful and pointless academic exercise and that learning to read is well within their grasp.

Remedial reading should probably be regarded more as convalescence than as curative.

DIALECT

Here is another source of individual difference that in principle should not have the slightest relevance for reading or learning to read but that has often considerable consequences for reading instruction. The whole notion that the dialect a person speaks is relevant to learning to read is based on the fable that written language represents a particular spoken dialect.

Written language is not the same as anyone's spoken language, for a number of good reasons that I discussed in Chapter 3. There is no reason to believe it necessary to speak a particular variety of spoken language in order to learn to read. On the contrary, written language should be easier for learning to read than attempts to imitate anyone's spoken dialect.

Part of the misunderstanding derives from a common confusion between the production and the comprehension of language. It's no more necessary that we should speak in a certain way in order to read than it is to speak a dialect in order to understand someone who is talking in it. We can all understand dialects that we can speak only imperfectly at best. People from different geographic regions of a country may speak quite differently, but this doesn't prevent them from making sense of the same national magazines and the same television programs. One great advantage of written language is that it cuts across dialects. People can understand each other's writing when they might find each other's speech difficult or impossible. The spelling of written words is not an exact representation of the sounds of anyone's spoken dialect, just as no one talks in the sentence structures of written language. Written language has its own characteristics and conventions that are in principle accessible to speakers of any dialect.

A concomitant of the frequent confusion between the language we produce and the language we comprehend, incidentally, is an unfortunate tendency to evaluate children's language ability, and even their capacity to learn, based on the way they speak. We all understand language that we couldn't possibly produce, and stressful circumstances can make us even more incoherent or tongue-tied. The only fair way to assess an individual's ability to comprehend language is to examine the language that the individual does in fact comprehend.

It's particularly unfair to evaluate a child's ability to comprehend in reading by the way in which the child reads aloud. Reading aloud is always more difficult than reading silently because on top of the basic task of making sense of the text is the added problem of identifying and articulating each individual word correctly. A child who reads aloud "Johnny ain't got no candy" when the text is *Johnny has no candy* is making sense of the print and reproducing it in a form that also makes sense to the child. It might only serve to confuse such a child to insist that the reading should be word perfect, especially at a first attempt. On the other hand, another child who gets every word right may not have the slightest idea of the meaning for the simple reason that the child wouldn't normally talk in that way.

But for many children in school, there is more to learning to read than making sense of print. There is also the matter of making sense of the instruction, and it's here that critical problems can occur. A teacher who requires children to master a particular dialect in order to make sense of the instruction is obviously going to find problems among speakers of other dialects. So is a teacher who unconsciously or otherwise rejects a child's dialect, or suggests that the dialect is inferior or in some way inadequate for the child's learning to read. Teachers should be aware of their own dialect; distinctions they think they observe may not, in fact, be part of their speech. Most of us feel we pronounce *caught, court,* and *cot* as three distinct sequences of sounds when, in fact, we probably do not. We may think we are saying "That word isn't *caught,* it's *cot,*" but if a child hears "That word isn't *court* it's *court,*" we're both likely to end up frustrated and confused. (The same applies to *merry, marry* and *Mary*, and many other groups of words that are distinctive in writing but not always in speech.)

Evidently, the extent to which teachers and pupils speak and comprehend different dialects is likely to have a bearing on how well the children will understand the instruction and how much they may become confused in learning to read. But the problem of dialect is minimized if reading is regarded as making sense of print and emphasis on word-perfect oral reading is reduced.

Some readers may object, "But shouldn't all children learn to speak good English?" (or "proper English"), which usually means a particular dialect. Perhaps so—this is another debatable issue, but it's not a matter that should be allowed to interfere with learning to read. Trying to change the way a child speaks during reading instruction can only serve to add intellectual and emotional strain, not to mention negative attitudes toward the teacher and education in general.

It is not, however, uncommon for reading to be confused with something else (like spoken language competence) or for children to be expected to learn reading and something else at the same time. Mathematics or social science teachers, for example, may complain that children don't read well enough to comprehend their texts or tests, when in fact what the children lack is comprehension of the subject matter. Perhaps certain children are inadequate in both respects; they are poor readers and they are also confused in the subject area. In that case the subject matter must be taught in some other way. Children won't advance in the subject area if they can't read the text, and they won't improve in their reading if the subject matter is opaque to them. The only solution for the teacher is to try to ensure that both reading and the subject matter are made as easy as possible, which means keeping them separate for the child having difficulty with both.

READING AND SPELLING

This is another case where the confusion of two quite distinct learning tasks can make both more difficult. It's sometimes argued that if children aren't taught to read by phonics, they will never learn to spell. But as we have seen, knowledge of phonics is not much help for spelling. The spelling-to-sound correspondences that are so unreliable for decoding written words to sound are equally misleading for trying to move from the sounds of speech to correct spelling. Children who spell "by ear" are the worst spellers; spelling is basically a matter of convention, with the best clues always provided by meaning. Words that have similar meanings tend to be spelled alike. It's no use trying to employ phonic rules to work out how *medicine* (*medisin?*) and *medical* (*medikal?*) are spelled; they share the same root meaning and thus the same spelling pattern. In the long run, spellings must be remembered, although the more words we already know, the easier it is to spell and to remember new spellings. That doesn't mean that children should be taught spelling from word lists—the thousands of words that most of us can spell were not learned 10 at a time from the word lists in our workbooks, but as a consequence of meaningful reading.

The second objection to the confusion of reading with spelling is that the more focused anyone is on individual letters and words during reading, the less will be learned about reading, and about spelling as well. The spellings of words are learned when they are encountered during meaningful reading, usually without conscious attention, just as spoken words are learned quite inconspicuously (especially by children) when they are encountered in meaningful situations. The more attention that is paid to spelling, the more the learner is likely to get anxious and resistant to "joining the spelling club," or to joining the literacy club as a whole.

I'm not suggesting that children shouldn't learn to spell correctly. On the contrary, it's by keeping concern for spelling clearly separate from the development of reading experience that children get the best opportunities to become fluent readers and spellers. Children can learn to read and write (and spell) concurrently, just as they learn to speak and comprehend spoken language at the same time. Learning about all aspects of language can be mutually supportive, although children should always be permitted to concentrate on one aspect at a time when they find it particularly helpful or interesting.

It's not necessary for teachers to feed instruction to children one spoonful at a time, and they have to be careful that children don't become confused or anxious because of inappropriate intervention. To make any aspect of language learning an issue—spelling, oral expression, written expression, neatness, even speed—when the child's concern is with a different aspect will interfere with both the teacher's and the child's intentions.

SUMMARY

Dyslexia is not a medical condition, seeing backwards is a physical impossibility, and "readiness" for reading is a mythical barrier. Many of the difficulties that some children experience when learning to read can be attributed to problems in the instruction, not problems in the learner.

Index

About the Author

Frank Smith is a writer and researcher living on Vancouver Island, British Columbia, Canada. He was born in England, took his under-graduate degree at the University of Western Australia, and has a Ph.D in psycholinguistics from Harvard University.

As a reporter and editor, he was on the staff of a number of news-papers and magazines in Europe and Australia. As a researcher, he has been associated with many projects concerned with literacy and language education. He was a professor at the Ontario Institute for Studies in Education and the Linguistics Department of the University of Toronto for 12 years, and subsequently was Lansdowne Professor of Language in Education at the University of Victoria, British Columbia, Canada. In 1992, he was distinguished visiting professor and head of the new Department of Applied English Language Studies at the University of the Witwatersrand in Johannesburg, South Africa.

Frank Smith has published short stories, poetry, a novel, and over 20 books concerned with language and education. They include *Ourselves: Why We Are Who We Are*, six editions of *Understanding Reading* and two editions of *Writing and the Writer*, published by Lawrence Erlbaum Associates; *Insult to Intelligence, Essays Into Literacy, Joining the Literacy Club, Between Hope and Havoc*, and *Unspeakable Acts, Unnatural Practices*, published by Heinemann Educational Books; and *Reading Without Nonsense* (four editions), *to think, The Glass Wall* (mathematics) and *The Book of Learning and Forgetting*, published by Teachers College Press.

He also co-edited *Awakening to Literacy* (Heinemann Educational Books) on the growth of children's awareness of written language, and *Whose Language? What Power?* (Teachers College Press) on the politics of second language teaching in South Africa.

His current research interests focus on the psychological, social, and cultural consequences of human technology, including language.